Garden Pools

Fountains & Waterfalls

By the Editors of Sunset Books and Sunset Magazine

LANE PUBLISHING CO. · MENLO PARK, CALIFORNIA

Foreword

The Victorians of England built palatial homes for goldfish. The Romans used stair-step pools and fountains to cool hot summer nights along the Mediterranean. The French used to spread out enormous sheets of water before their chateaux. Europe's great gardens of almost every age have preserved the royal tradition of luxuriant pools, fountains, and waterfalls.

Although maintaining gardens on so grand a scale is somewhat less practical in modern cities and suburbs, the basic ideas behind pools and fountains of earlier times are as valid today as ever. The orderliness of the formal garden is still attractive to many contemporary homeowners. Gracefully proportioned geometric shapes can produce an air of serenity in a garden. Careful selection of materials can recapture something of another era or match the utilitarian features of modern architecture. A garden pool is a natural starting place for designing a new garden or for redesigning an older one—an enchanting place for guests to visit.

Goldfish or koi dimpling the waters of a pool are still a captivating sight. The cooling effect of moving water on hot, dry summer days and evenings is as welcome as ever. Quiet and reflecting, or dancing and image-shattering—water brings charm and beauty into a garden. Whether it reflects the sky and clouds, a piece of garden sculpture, or the arching branch of a nearby tree, water creates an ever-changing picture.

Water brings luster to tile, brick, wood, concrete, stone, and plants when they become wet. Anyone who has collected gem-like wet pebbles, then watched them change to dull, dry, very ordinary looking rocks understands the transforming character of water. A garden pool is an ideal showcase for a collection of rocks or shells that show their best colors when they are in water. And the bottom of a shallow pool is an excellent place to display handsome mosaics.

For gardeners, a garden pool opens up a whole new world. Long accustomed to the frequent problem of providing adequate drainage for plants, pool owners face an entirely different form of gardening in which plants thrive on water alone. Water plants add new colors, shapes, and textures to a garden, especially the hardy and tropical water lilies, oxygenating plants and grasses, and such floating plants as the water hyacinth.

Edited by John Gillespie

Design: Mike Rogondino, Joe Seney
Cover: The engineering is professional, but the design, construction, rock placement and plantings are the work of owners, the Mark Schmeekles of San Mateo, California. This was their first project. Photographed by George Selland, Moss Photography.

Editor, Sunset Books: David E. Clark

Ninth Printing August 1981

Contents

Unusual fountain *recirculates swimming pool water through circular fountain head and large central jet. With fountain turned off, pool becomes hydromassage unit. Landscape Architects: Richard E. Jones, Robert D. Peterson.*

Fountains

Water in motion is nearly always dramatic, and a flowing fountain introduces water as a star performer in the garden scene. But a fountain does more practical work than merely entertain with colorful sights and musical sounds. During the hot, dry days of summer, it fills the air with moisture, providing a cool garden retreat for you, your family, and guests.

Fountains that spray, fountains that spill, and fountains that splash are the three basic types. Spray fountains are made versatile by fountain heads (see page 77) that send water upward in shapes ranging from massive columns to sprays as delicate as lace. Spill fountains generally take the form of tiers of spill pans or wall fountains. Splash fountains can contain either sprays or spills, but only in a splash fountain is water interrupted by a piece of sculpture.

Various fountain heads and spray or spill fountains can be purchased directly from the manufacturer or from garden supply, plumbing, and hardware stores. Splash fountains, on the other hand, are nearly always custom designed, either by the homeowner or by a landscape architect.

Fountain design and location

The main rule in spray fountain design is this: use a short, heavy column of water in windy spots; go for height, distance, or drama only where the spray will not blow widely, drenching spectators. Spill fountains, because of their customary design and sheltered location, do not usually present a wind problem.

With a little help from an array of available fountain heads, water can be sculpted into all kinds of fanciful shapes. The simplest fountain form is a single jet of water rising gracefully from a pool and falling, rainlike, back into it. Its fine spray falls musically on water as a light rain falls on a lake. The jet may be a short, burbling column suggesting a small underground spring, or it may be obviously manmade—an arching stream falling in the center of a pool.

Professional designers try to position a fountain against a background that dramatizes the water's movement. Water in a heavy column tends to be translucent, so backgrounds ought to be dark. Fine sprays usually appear best when outlined against a flat surface. Heavy sprays are dominating and will stand out even against a lacy bower of leaves.

Installation

When you choose moving water for your garden in preference to still water, the plumbing becomes more complex. And if you plan to include fish and plants in your pool (see pages 52–65), you should plan the installation very carefully.

The simplest, easiest, and most economical method of installing a fountain is to purchase a complete unit at a retail outlet or directly from the manufacturer (see drawing, page 77). The manufactured models are precisely engineered, guaranteed for a year or more, and come in a variety of sizes with optional components. No plumbing is required. You simply put the kit together, fill the bowl with water, and connect the fountain unit to an electric power source. Fiberglass bowl sizes are 36 through 94 inches in diameter. The fountain units contain a motor, pump, strainer, valve, leveling device, lights, and fountain head, all mounted in a single compact submersible base. Timers and color blenders for lighting that are programmed to automatic sequences can also be purchased.

Natural pool has large open jet located slightly above water's surface. Fountain recirculates water from a small manmade lake; pool flows into lake. Statue surrounded by sculptured evergreen shrubs creates special fountain effect. Landscape Architect: Charles Darland.

The spray's the thing

Basically, a spray fountain uses water in opposition to gravity, sometimes for picturesque water patterns, sometimes to interact with sculpture, and, on occasion, simply for the sight and sound of falling water.

Here are the basic types of spray fountains:

- A short, heavy, burbling column of water rising vertically from an open inlet pipe below the pool's surface.
- A burbling column of water from an open inlet pipe above the pool's surface. This column rises higher than one that begins below the pool's surface.
- A fine, forceful spray coming from an inlet pipe having a spray jet smaller than the pipe's diameter. The spray rises vertically, describes a graceful arc, or rotates—depending upon the fountain head's design. Some designs have both rotating and stationary sprays.
- Moving sprays similar to the operation of lawn sprinklers.

Two design limitations apply to the fountains described above: 1) If fine sprays are too translucent, heighten their dramatic impact by posing them against a dark background; 2) As water rises higher, the pool diameter must increase proportionately; otherwise, a steady loss occurs as the water falls, especially in a windy garden. Water loss, however, can be largely reduced by installing a splash screen. (Retail stores do not generally stock these; they must be ordered from the manufacturer.)

Spray rises *from natural pool that was specifically designed to contrast with contemporary patio. Fountain head can be replaced to change spray to different pattern. Overflow pipe at right of fountain head carries off excess water during rainy season. Landscape Architect: Lawrence Halprin.*

Oasislike retreat *surrounds fountain with tall spray pattern. Recirculating pump is submersible type. Gravel and cactus plants in foreground suggest desert scene. Plants in and around pool create tropical contrast to cactus. Bench invites cool relaxation on warm days. Landscape Architect: Lawrence Halprin.*

Fragmented droplets *rise from rotating fountain head in Sunset's patio at Menlo Park, California; fountain is located at end of pool to allow sitting on pool's border-bench. Recirculation is accomplished by tiny pump located below drain. Potted accent plants on bench and boxed horsetail plant in fountain pool harmonize with patio design. Landscape Architect: Thomas Church.*

Accent spray fountain *provides needed airborne moisture for surrounding water, bog, and background plants. Fountain, white metal bowl, rocks, and clear plastic floats draw attention to this section of garden. Fountain can be moved by detaching fountain head and hose (set underneath bowl and hidden by plants). Tiny water spray is powered by 1/55 horsepower pump.*

Another burbler *pushes shallow column upward from rustic pool converging into small, tumbling garden stream. Open pipe fountain head located slightly below surface simulates an underground spring, suits this suburban setting better than typical fine spray head. The pump requires 1-horsepower motor.*

Portable display fountain *for contemporary gardens is ideal for showing off water lily blossoms, gardenias, hyacinths, or other floating blooms. Plumbing for this unit is ultra-simplified: smallest type of manufactured pump is attached to bottom of the plastic pan. Pan rests on frame designed for this pool.*

Random streams *spurt from professional design made of easily workable copper tubing welded to a custom designed fountain head. Special nozzles produce whimsical jet patterns. Commercially available metal saucer is specially treated to prevent rust but requires regular cleaning to control algae. Landscape Architects: Eckbo, Royston, and Williams.*

Dry-country spa *provides cooling relief from desert view. You can see fountain from entry, hear it from bedroom and patio. Rocks and plants provide vertical contrasts. Fountain is made from reinforced concrete faced with mortar to simulate water eddies. Fountain head and tiny pump are typical units available in most hardware stores. Architect: Bennie M. Gonzales.*

Rock mosaic *lines concrete pedestal fountain. Wood template was used to make concrete mold on sand base. (See "They built a fountain on a pile of sand," page 12.) Thin layer of concrete was then spread over sand; next, wire mesh was laid to reinforce concrete; more concrete was added to attain desired thickness; template was then used to achieve smooth inner surface for bowl. Mosaic was laid in mortar on finished bowl. (See "Mosaics from pebbles and shells," page 76.) Fountain head is ordinary commercial type. Architect: Georg Hoy.*

Fountain head design *and spray pattern shown here are typical of those available in hardware stores and garden supply centers. Units for private gardens are usually smaller, use pumps with less horsepower. This fountain is heavy duty commercial type, takes a 2¼-horsepower pump. Complete fountain kits or separate fountain components can be purchased. Kits contain fountain head (optional variety of sprays), filter, pump, programmed lighting sequences, fountain bowls, splash screens, and fountain stabilizers.*

Two-in-one *circle-spray fountain is enhanced by traditional European cherub statue and warm brick tones of pool walls. This fountain head is commercially available. Standard pool construction included building forms reinforced with steel rods and wire mesh for pouring 6-inch-thick concrete shell. Brick facing was added after concrete had set. For cleaning, drain empties pool into ravine beyond trees in background. Landscape Architect: Thomas Church.*

Dramatic simplicity is demonstrated in three professionally designed fountains. **Upper left:** The arcing symmetry of large central fountain and formal arrangement of 6 smaller sprays contrasts with random stone pattern of building and natural landscaping. The display commands immediate attention of visitors. **Upper right:** three vertical fountains imitate row of tall trees in background. **Lower left:** the small garden pool has rotating fountain head; spray suggests plant foliage and contrasts with sharp geometric design of pebbled concrete pool, steps, and walk. Requirements for each fountain are basically similar—an adequate pump and a fountain head designed for type of spray desired. Upper left and right: Rainjet design. Lower left: Jack W. Butenica, Landscape Architect.

They built a fountain on a pile of sand

This graceful raised fountain cost its builder a pile of sand, a wooden template, about $100 worth of building materials, and a weekend of diligent work.

The required materials are these: 420 pounds of cement (white cement can be obtained for a premium price), two tons of builder's sand, 600 pounds of ½-inch pea gravel, 10 feet of ⅜-inch copper pipe, 10 feet of ½-inch copper pipe (both of these may vary, depending on the pump's location), a 5-gallon watertight container to hold the pump, a 60-cycle submersible pump, and 40 feet of ½-inch steel rods.

Also needed: a 3-foot length of 1 by 4-inch lumber, a 7 by 10-inch piece of ¾-inch plywood, two 4-inch mending plates, and two small cans of the kind used for frozen concentrates of fruit juices.

Piping and footing. After locating the fountain, the first task is to set the pipes in the ground and pour part of the footing.

The footing is a block of concrete about 2 feet square. It prevents the fountain from tipping. Dig the footing hole about 14 inches deep. At the same time, dig a trench for the pipes from the footing hole to the point where the pump will go.

Bend the pipes to a 90-degree angle, taking care not to make the corner too abrupt. The vertical section of the pipes should be long enough so it will stick up 3 inches above the finished floor of the pool.

Lay the pipes in the trench. Check the vertical section with a spirit level to make sure it is perpendicular. (Otherwise, the template will not work correctly.)

Mix enough concrete to fill the bottom 8 inches of the footing hole. Allow concrete to harden overnight so pipes will offer a solid pivot to the template.

Template and reinforcing. While the concrete is setting, the template can be made (see step 3) and the reinforcing rods cut and bent.

As reinforcement, this design calls for eight 3-foot sections, each bent to match the template, and two circular rods. One of the circular rods should fall 3 inches from the edge. The other should be about one-third the circumference (circumference = radius × 6.2148).

Building the mold. The second day, pour the remaining 6 inches of the footing, bringing it to ground level. Make this portion of the mix dry enough to support the weight of the sand, but soft enough to receive the reinforcing rods at a later stage.

Now, build the mold by piling wet sand under the template, keeping even on all sides at all stages. Keep the sand wet and compact it with hand pats or by jogging the template.

Pouring the concrete. Mix the concrete: 1 part cement, 1 part sand, 1 part gravel, and about 1 gallon of water to each 100 pounds of aggregate.

Remove the template; pour concrete into the middle of the mold, over the footing area. Trowel from center to edge in one direction only, so sand is not disturbed. Cover the entire mold with a 1-inch layer of concrete. Embed the steel rods in a spoke pattern. Put the circular rods down, wiring them to spokes with light wire and keeping the whole assembly flat. Pour another 1-inch layer of concrete over the reinforcing grille. Remove the bottom section of the template and use the straight edge of the top to smooth the bowl.

Trim edges smooth before the concrete sets.

Keep the fountain damp for two days while the concrete sets. When it has set, fit the fountain head on the feed pipe. In this case, the designer used a threaded pipe cap, with three holes drilled to receive three lengths of ³/₁₆-inch copper tubes that were welded in place and fitted with nozzles.

Cut the ½-inch return pipe to water level; cover it with a copper screen to filter out dirt.

The pump is connected at the other end according to manufacturer's specifications.

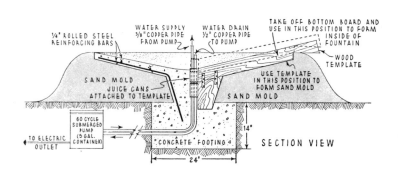

1. **Mark circumference** *of pool with chalk, break out hole for footing. Hole should be 24 by 24 inches.*

2. Using scribed circle, *cut and bend reinforcing rods to fit the chalk-marked radius described in text at left.*

3. Small frozen juice cans *make a suitable sleeve for the template to revolve upon. Cans should fit pipe closely.*

4. Excavate *for pipes and footing 14 inches deep, 24 by 24 inches square. Seat pipes; then pour footing.*

5. Build sand mold, *using template to achieve the shape. Axis should be precisely vertical to avoid tilted pool.*

6. Pour concrete *to half the thickness of pool; then embed reinforcing rods. Intersections should be wired.*

7. Finish pour. *Remove ear from template. Use it to make either rippled or smooth surface on inside of bowl.*

8. Huge sand mold *produces rough-hewn but gracefully proportioned fountain. Design: Virginia Davidson*

Corner grotto *created from simple materials. Covered board houses water inlet; spill pan is boiler end; large pool was purchased from garden supply center. Background is rolled lath fencing material. Located beneath bowl is ¼ horsepower pump. Design: Henry Van Siegman.*

Spill fountains

Whether a spill fountain is an ordinary household pipe pouring water into a container, a series of spill pans attached to a wall, or a scaled-down version of the great Roman ornamental fountains, it is nearly always designed to capture a specific characteristic of falling water or create a particular tableau. For some people, the simple sound of falling water is adequate; others may want their fountain to carry a symbolic message in its design. Rarely is an attempt made to disguise the water source or to make the fountain appear to be a waterfall. No fountain head is used at the inlet for a fountain of falling water.

Simple spill fountains

The simplest spill fountain design, and the least expensive, is a single stream of water pouring into a pool or container. The pool can be large or small, depending on the space and budget allotted to it. When containers are small enough to be portable, though, they cease to be fountains and become decorative water accents for the garden.

(Continued on page 16)

Rugged looking basin *is a concrete shell poured beside existing large boulders. Owner decided it was easier to create the fountain than remove the heavy stones. Hose is attached to pump; other end is braced between rocks. Rushes, horsetail plant, small tree, and creekbed rocks complete the scene. Design: Leon Frehner.*

Almost any pipe *or water inlet can be used to create a fountain. Here, no pump is used. Miniature flow of tap water into pool keeps moisture-loving plants well supplied. Combination of pebbles and trickling sound of water suggest small stream in rustic Japanese style garden. Design: Tats Ishimoto.*

Metal spill pans *are available in a variety of forms and materials at garden and building supply centers and hardware stores. Kits containing spill pans, recirculating pump, and hose are available in plastic and metal. Plastic designs come in various colors. Unit shown here is made of metal. Design: Wegman/Offenhauser.*

Recirculation pipe *is attached behind the wall to bottom of overflowing bowl. Water splashes noisily on porous lava rock in seminaturalistic pool. Horsetail plant is in planter box disguised by rocks. Pool drains into pump located near wall. Wall also supports bank in background. Landscape Architect: Courtland Paul.*

Fountains **15**

Watering wall *provides trickling sound and practicality; it waters moisture-loving plants around bowl. Lack of drain requires this solution to overflow problem. Fountain is supplied from garden water line. Bowl rests on stone projection from base of wall. Construction required meticulous work with mortar and natural stone. Design: H. P. Weldman.*

Spill pans are available in two and three-tiered plastic or metal sets that you can purchase at hardware or department stores and at garden supply centers. If you are a skilled craftsman, you can make your own spill fountain from boiler ends or build a series of spill pans from your own materials and design.

More ambitious: wall fountains

Wall fountains acted as very practical public water sources long before the invention of indoor plumbing. The ancient form is seen frequently in Europe, most often along the Mediterranean coast. Water passing through a sculptured figure standing in a wall niche was usually employed to fill a servant's water jar.

Today, the fountain's principal role—ornamental—remains. A wall fountain in a private garden continues the old world style but not its practicality. Submersible pumps and water pipes can be combined to add a fountain to an existing wall. Construction is much simpler, though, if a pump can be

Expanse of moving water *can cool the patio in desert country. Recirculating pump moves water from lower pool (left) to spill pan on top of wall. Main pool overflow courses through drain tiles set in brick wall and descends to lower pool. Design: Guy Green.*

Half-circle form *of pool and triangular spill pans dominate modular design of patio. Metal sheets are offset, flow directly into pool; equalizing valve attached to pump's pipe connection controls balanced flow of water. Custom spill pans are product of sheet metal shop. Architects: Osmundson/Staley.*

Water trays *of the fountain, white brick wall, bricks, and mosaic-covered pool floor are all rectangles, as are the planter boxes and the patio itself. Water falls in even pattern from tray to tray. Pool drain and recirculating pump are at upper left of pool. Architects: Williams & Williams.*

Cooling sound *surrounds triple cascade of wall, tiers, and spill fountain. Floral accents provided by horsetail plant (at left in upper pool) and water lilies complement rectangular sandstone wall lined with tile. Although water volume appears large, small pump does adequate job for this type of fountain.*

incorporated into a wall as the fountain is being built. Placing of the water inlet is a matter of personal preference. It can pour directly into the pool from the pipe, overflow from a basin, or flow indirectly from a series of spill pans or trays.

Building a formal or classic wall fountain is relatively expensive. If it is to look its best, it should be set in a very large area and be designed by a landscape architect. Not only is the formal fountain itself an extensive project but also the surrounding area must have complementary garden features if the fountain is to fit into its environment.

Home-crafted fountain (left) is made from lightweight vermiculite concrete (2 : 2 : 3 formula) reinforced with metal mesh and ¼-inch steel rods, was cast as slab on back with 3-dimensional grille on top. Design: Clyde Childress. **Top right:** classic European wall fountain design has changed very little over many centuries. Here, typical cherub sculpture pours stream into Spanish-tiled pool. Presence of recirculation pump substitutes for old style village or neighborhood well. **Lower right:** in this wall fountain the same principle operates as in European village fountains.

A three-tiered geometric fountain

Here is a project for a man with woodworking skill—and confidence. Plywood forms were used so the corners would be precisely sharp.

Materials and techniques. As the sketch above indicates, fitting the legs to the main pool form was an exacting task. Then, too, the forms of ½-inch plywood needed considerable shoring up to bear the weight of the concrete even though a lightweight aggregate was used.

The formula was 2 parts cement, 2 parts sand, 1 part fire clay, and 4 parts aggregate. The aggregate was 2 parts ⅜-inch haydite to 1 part fine gravel.

Over this the craftsman applied a finish coat of 1 : 1 sand-cement to assure the fountain's being waterproof. This coat also contained about ¼-pound of integral dye to color the finished product.

Zinc flashing, applied with mastic, protects the wooden post against deterioration. The ¾-inch galvanized pipe supports and drains for the two upper pools were cast right in the concrete.

How it works. Water is pumped to the top of the upper pipe and flows down through the pipe to drilled holes near surface level in the top pool. The water flows from pool to pool until it reaches the lowest one. From there it drains through a tube (buried in the planting bed) to the recirculating pump.

The roundabout system was designed to retain the free-floating appearance of the upper two pools.

Fine geometrical sense *produced this basic idea, meticulous attention to detail created the plans, and carpentry skill brought the fountain into being. Each six-sided bowl is one-third larger than the bowl above. Lightweight aggregate was used in mixing concrete. Lower pool is cast around post, upper one around pipe for water from recirculating pump. Design: Charles B. Shaw.*

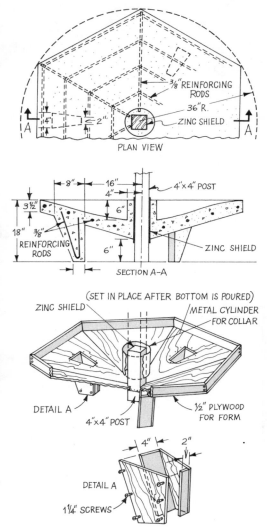

Water sprays *from both sides of perforated pipe and then through evenly spaced holes or over edge of plastic sheet. Rippling shadows result from underwater light placed to play on sheet. Low voltage fixtures are found in most hardware stores. Design: Glen Hunt.*

Splash sculpture

The wide range of designs for splash sculpture fountains suggests a long history. For centuries, pumping water up through a sculpture to have it splash over a series of surfaces into a pool has been a favored form for fountains. Traditionally, the water inlet was a Grecian urn or other art object, held by a cherubic-looking nymph or symbolic figure. Nearly every city in Europe has a public square that displays some variation of the splash sculpture fountain style.

Remember, though, that a formal fountain requires lots of room. If you want to place a splash sculpture fountain where space is limited, you can scale down the design. A metal sculpture gives a strong contemporary appearance. Avoid using a traditional stone sculpture in a modern pool; artistic balance is a tricky accomplishment.

You will find both traditional and modern sculptures in stone and metal on sale at garden supply centers, stone cutting yards, and import stores. A few department stores in some communities also stock them. Both stone and metal sculptures can be commissioned, usually at the studio of the artist or at a gallery acting as the artist's agent.

Falling water *takes creative detours in these three fountains.* **Top left:** *mid-lawn fountain has sculpture mounted above fountain head; spray bounces from metal birds formed in various attitudes of flight. Fountain sometimes attracts wild birds.* **Top right:** *water splashes downward over irregular stone shapes, each with a hole drilled into it. Stones are fitted over a central pipe, allowed to hang randomly. Rocks in the pool supplement splashing action.* **Bottom:** *here's a sculpture of free form concrete with inlet pipe extended up through the center, placing the fountain head 12 inches above the sculpture.*

Cool, clear water *runs over falls at rate of 18 gallons per minute. Powered by 1-horsepower pump with semi-automatic filter system, pool never needs cleaning. Design: Herb Simon.*

Waterfalls and Streams

Whether the sight is one of nature's awesome cascades at Yosemite National Park or a simple mountain stream falling over rustic terraces toward the sea, nearly everyone stops to watch a waterfall. The enchantment of flowing water is so pervasive that people often travel hundreds of miles to see it.

Inspired by such visits with nature but unable to arrange for them as often as we would like, we can compensate by building naturalistic waterfalls of varying sizes in our gardens, indoor-outdoor rooms, atriums—even in our living rooms.

Natural waterfalls

Some of these waterfalls are obviously manmade—tending to geometric shapes that imitate the urban environment. But most waterfall builders prefer to imitate nature. They've learned that native waterfalls take the kind of tumble that looks proper in a home garden.

If you have not already done so, you can obtain a wealth of information and inspiration (*and* a pleasant holiday) from a research trip into a wilderness area where streams are in abundance. Or visit a landscape architect and tell him that you'd like to see some garden waterfall designs.

Observation and careful planning are essential to building a waterfall that will appear to be a product of nature. Generally, soil, various-sized pebbles and stone, and appropriate plants are the ingredients. Parts of a waterfall to be concealed include the concrete shell of the pool, the mortar for the stones if you use it, and the pump and plumbing installation for recirculating the water.

Waterfalls for easy installation are sold by pump and fountain manufacturers. You can also buy simulated rock that appears almost realistic. Viewed from across a room, the waterfall can appear very realistic, but such installations do not invite close scrutiny.

Natural streams

What is a natural stream in the western context? This is not an easy question to answer. There are many varieties—rushing streams on granite mountains, lazy streams in upland meadows, and muddy streams in farm valleys, ranging in size from a tiny trickle to awesome rapids.

In a private garden, a "natural" stream ought to provide the kind of flow that your property can handle easily. Unless your stream burbles mysteriously out of the ground, the rushing water usually has a waterfall as its source. In this case, the water must be piped from where the stream ends (perhaps where it flows into a pool) back to the waterfall, where it begins its journey again.

If you are fortunate enough to have a natural stream running across your property, you've already saved construction time and expense. But if you want to change the stream in any way, be sure to contact the Department of Fish and Game in your state. Laws govern all stream changes, and the laws are very strictly enforced.

Lessons learned *from natural waterfall* **(left)** *are applied to manmade falls* **(right).** *Note that rocks are placed to accommodate natural flow of water. Trees, plants, and loose soil are at side, never directly in path of moving water. Design: Herb Simon.*

Natural waterfall design

How do you build a natural-looking waterfall? Carefully observe the way nature builds hers:

• Stubborn flat rocks fortify the center of the stream, forming the edge of the falls.

• Relentlessly the press of water rushes along lines of least resistance, between, around, and over the firmly entrenched stones, washing away the dirt, bits of gravel, and all other loose material.

• Nature frames the falling water's path with stones cast aside or worn away by the rushing water and with appropriate plantings.

To begin planning a ''natural'' waterfall, make some preliminary drawings or rough sketches. If you have questions, talk them over with a landscape architect or professional builder. Visual plans will help to reduce the number of construction problems that you may encounter later. If you decide to build a natural-looking waterfall, study the combination of balanced native stones and free-form concrete.

In the mountainous West, native stone and natural water are a combination that is everywhere at hand. Unless you plan to scale the entire project to a smaller size, the following general rule seems to apply: wherever native stone is to play a dominant part in a garden waterfall, ample space is a fundamental

Small basins *in setting of large boulders recall a mountain spring. When you design such a setting, water must appear to follow lines of least resistence. It should not appear or disappear abruptly if you expect to imitate nature accurately. Design: Lawrence Underhill.*

Another tiny flow *of water —but this time the water falls into a small stream that disappears gradually through landscaped tunnel, where pump sends it back to source of waterfall. On a hillside, you can let gravity do its work. Design: Lawrence Underhill.*

This waterfall *was built in casual, pebble-lined concrete pool; total project included locally found stones, 3 bags of purchased pebbles, cement, lumber for a bridge (see page 51). All plants were moved from other parts of the yard. Children play in the pool without harming it.*

Without the fence *in background, this could appear to be a real mountain stream. Stones are artfully placed to imitate nature, foliage is off to the side, and rivulets of water pursue a naturally rugged path of least resistance.*

requirement. Boulders fill up space quickly, and the shell of the pool itself has to be sizable to remain in scale with the stones. Some types of stone—mainly the shales and other striated types—can be stacked in ways that look natural. Massive stones, such as the granites so common in western mountains, look far less at home when stacked.

By paying close attention to scale, it is possible to build a bustling small waterfall from a tiny volume of water. Fist-sized broken stones can be arranged to appear much larger. Dwarf varieties of native plants can be transformed by creative imagination into their standard-sized counterparts.

Constructing the falls

Construction of the falls is the simplest part of designing a natural-looking waterfall. Getting the surrounding materials into harmony is work that demands close observation and careful planning. Basically, the idea is to separate two or more pools at different heights so that they will appear to have been formed without man's interference. A torrential waterfall with its source mysteriously placed midway up a property line fence is not likely to appear credible. The twin keys to success are stones placed in harmony with their environment, and appropriate plantings.

Structurally, keep three important points in mind: 1) the upper pool is usually the smaller of the two, just large enough to achieve a bustling flow of

Harmoniously combined *natural and contemporary pool designs each retain individuality; each is made of reinforced concrete. Contemporary upper pool is lined with firebrick. Lower pool edge is disguised by bog and water plants. Detailed natural section rivals forest brook.*

Genuine stream *in back yard is rare good fortune seldom found in garden areas. Any changes made in stream's path should first be cleared by state fish and game officials. Remember also to keep all changes in scale with rest of stream to avoid upsetting nature's balance.*

Musical trickle *falls into natural-appearing pool from 60-foot garden stream running alongside house (not shown). Small recirculating pump carries water 8 feet up and back to source of stream at rate of 500 gallons per hour. Pool has gravel overflow bed. Design: Michael Wills.*

Close study *of natural formations in Rocky Mountain states produced realistic stream. Swimming pool pump is required to move the volume of water rushing over short, rugged course. Small trees planted nearby will grow very tall. Design: Hersaal L. Pitts.*

water; 2) the entire face of the falls must be sealed to prevent dirt from washing into the lower pool under pressure from the moving water; 3) the floor of the lower pool directly beneath the falls should be at least twice as thick as the normal floor. Falling water exerts a tremendous scouring force. Its point of entry into the lower pool should be at the place where the pool is deepest.

Mortaring the interstices between stones, unless done with great skill, will be evident. Without mortaring, you must resign yourself to a certain amount of soil washing into the water with each rain. But if the pool contains plants, it will not be completely clear in any case. Similarly, the face of the waterfall should be watertight. Otherwise, ground water will seep through and discolor the water.

Water in arid land, *particularly running water, commands immediate attention. A garden waterfall is so rare that its presence becomes utterly luxurious, almost hypnotic in its sight and sound. Design shown creates casual impression of nature transferred from another climate, placed artistically where view includes both water and a thirsty land. Concrete shell has wire mesh reinforcing, submerged pump provides recirculation, rocks are imported river stone, gravel is pulverized desert stone. Design: Louise Bell.*

Impressions of nature, *rather than detailed imitations, these three waterfalls create individual designs for patios.* **Top left:** *natural rock, plants, and falling water contrast with sharp angles of pool overhead structure. Design: Guy Greene.* **Top right:** *water pouring from rock simulates underground spring or artesian effect. Grottolike pool is set off by container plants.* **Left:** *vigorously rushing water cools warm patio; falls recirculate 18 gallons per minute. Design: L. Raymond Hodges.*

It gurgles like an underground spring

Here is one of the easiest ways to make a small, informal or natural pool containing a waterfall.

The builder used a fairly stiff mix of 1 part cement, 2 parts sand, and 3 parts gravel. The pool is poured in one continuous operation, and since the sides approach closely a slope of 45 degrees, concrete has to be stiff to stay in place.

The mix is troweled into shape as it is poured. In this case, the builder started at the tip so he could work carefully toward the drain and inlet pipes (the inlet pipe was capped with plastic to keep it clean during the building process).

To aid the natural appearance, the pool surface was covered with a rock mosaic, which was set in place while the concrete was still plastic. The mosaic extends from the edge of the pool to the bottom curve of the wall; the floor was left exposed and rough.

This pool is located in a mild-winter area, so its builder did not take the precautionary step of putting down a 3 to 4-inch layer of compacted gravel as a base for his concrete shell. In cold areas, this technique will minimize the thaw season possibility of heaving and settling soil, which can cause even reinforced concrete to crack.

The excavation was made with care so that the concrete rested on firmly compacted soil. Trenches for pipes were kept as small as possible, and they were filled with gravel. (A recirculating pump produces the small waterfall; its system is separate from the drain, which is controlled by a valve outside the pool.)

Water gurgles cheerfully *through fissure in stone wall behind this pool. Medium-sized recirculating pump creates flow suggesting underground spring. Waterfall's proximity to hills lends credibility to design. Owner excavated, installed plumbing, poured concrete, and created rock mosaic before constructing stone wall. When landscaping is complete, mature plants will mask raw edge of pool, which was made purposely higher than grade-level to prevent mud from washing into water. Landscape Architect: Lawrence Halprin.*

1. **Measure area** for pool excavation. Dig hole to desired depth; dig narrow trenches at bottom for drain pipe (plugged to keep out dirt). Install pump, drain pipes in trenches; be sure that water runs downward into pump (unless you are using a submersible type of pump). Attention to detail is vital to function of waterfall.

2. **Cover pipe** and trenches firmly, excluding drain hole. Install curved outer form of staked hardboard (or your own design) and brace at waterfall end. Tamp earth floor to shape desired. Remove plug from drain and install drain-grate (this marks level of finished pool floor). Note waterfall inlet pipe at right; wall will enclose it.

3. **Prepare** stiff mix of concrete (see text, page 30) and assemble all tools needed for forming pool floor and walls. Because of step 4, concrete must be poured and troweled to rough finish as quickly as possible. Here, builder positions large rock after troweling concrete. Note drain-grate level and relation of rock to inlet pipe.

4. **Rock mosaic** requires careful planning and some fast handwork if you are to stay ahead of the setting concrete. Lay out pebbles and rocks before you pour and trowel the pool shell. Or have a helper sort out rocks as you press them into the wall. When mosaic is completed, check pool and grade level relationship.

Small moat *encircles patio, providing an island in the sun for peace and quiet. Recirculating pump is hidden in rock cairn at upper right, keeps water moving slowly by means of small but vigorous waterfall. Streambed is concrete. Design: Mario Acevedo.*

Would you like to build a stream?

Natural streams are as individually different as any of nature's other creations. Before building a garden stream, a homeowner would be wise to settle on a single model drawn from his own experience. Streams designed only by imagination tend to encounter difficulties with nature's laws. Mark Twain expressed such an admonition in *"Fenimore Cooper's Literary Offenses,"* from which the following excerpt is taken:

"In the *Deerslayer* tale Cooper has a stream which is fifty feet wide where it flows out of a lake; it presently narrows to twenty as it meanders along for no given reason, and yet when a stream acts like that it ought to be required to explain itself. Fourteen pages later the width of the brook's outlet from the lake has suddenly shrunk thirty feet and becomes 'the narrowest part of the stream.' This shrinkage is not accounted for. The stream has bends in it, a sure indication that it has alluvial banks and cuts them, yet these bends are only thirty and fifty feet long. If Cooper had been a nice and punctilious observer he would have noticed that the bends were oftener nine hundred feet long than short of it."

Despite Fenimore Cooper's embarrassment, Mark Twain's criticism is soundly based on observations of slow streams and contains a lesson for anyone planning to build a stream.

Water moving at a languid pace will wander through curves, always washing the outside bank of the curve. Streams, therefore, tend to grow wider at the

Scale is always important *when designing a Japanese-style garden. This entire garden area is only 25 by 25 feet. Stones appear large but would not strain a good college shot putter. Pebbles and ever-present oriental lantern are typical Nipponese design signatures. Stream border is natural arrangement. Design: Tats Ishimoto.*

Filtering stream *purifies swimming pool water as it travels over extensive pebbled concrete course through garden area. Pool pump is over-size because of distance that water must be carried. Stream originates as waterfall at top center of garden.*

Beginning and end *of stream's action resides in pump located in cluster of rocks. Water has to be lifted only 1 foot to waterfall. A watertight wall separates terminal pool and headwaters of stream. Bordering bog plants are fed directly by the slow-moving stream. Design: Mario Acevedo.*

midpoint of a curve. They become shallower along the inside because water moves more slowly along the inside curve and silt is deposited at that point.

A fast stream rushes in a fairly straight line, detouring only where rocks bar its path. The rapidly moving water tends to keep such a stream bed free of mud.

The choice between a slow or a fast moving stream depends upon the topography of your land and may be entirely governed by the landscaping requirements of the site.

Taming a natural stream

Perhaps you own, or are thinking of buying, a piece of land with a stream already on it, and you would like to do something with it other than watch it rushing past the back door. Possibly you can build a waterfall. This involves engineering problems that will probably require professional skill. It is often necessary to build a dam to back water up high enough to create a waterfall.

If the stream is used by spawning salmon, a homeowner is required by law to obtain a building permit from his State Department of Fish and Game and to have the site inspected before any construction work is begun. In some cases, the homeowner will have to build a fish ladder (a series of progressive pools) to compensate for changes that would block the passage of spawning fish or keep newly hatched fish from swimming to the sea.

In redesigning the bed or course of a natural stream, great care should be taken to keep each changed factor in scale with the rest of the stream bed. Oversights can be disastrous. Note where currents will work against soft banks and the extent of scouring action if you change the course of the stream; in time it may chart a third course to your great distress. Flooding a pool to start a waterfall may bring the water level to a point at which it can exert force against a weak spot left unguarded.

You can get detailed information about state laws, as well as some how-to-do-it information, by writing to the engineering section of the State Department of Fish and Game in your state capital.

A drainage problem *created this garden stream at the foot of a steep bank. Since the surface flow could not be prevented, it was channeled along perimeter of lawn. So attractive was the result that owners added a water line to keep the flow going at the end of the rainy season, creating marshy area for bog plants. Design: John Caitlin.*

Simplicity *is the keynote in this pool design. Gravel, and choice plant material— used with restraint and placed with care— combine effectively to form a pleasant natural setting. Design: Sierra Madre Garden Club.*

Garden Pools

The size and shape of a garden pool can be as uniquely designed as the owner's imagination permits. For do-it-yourself designers, however, the best rule is this: keep it simple. Complex designs are not only difficult to manage during construction but also rarely achieve the effect hoped for.

You may want to choose from among these possibilities: a small decorative pool, a formal pool, or a natural pool. If you want to start small, there are tiny decorative garden pools that have the advantages of being both portable and versatile. You can pick them up at garden supply and statuary stores, scavenge about your home for such items as an old wooden tub or a glass fiber bowl, or create small pools from such materials as vermiculite concrete or waterproofed wood. You can also change the accent in your garden by relocating a pool from time to time. You can leave it in its rough state or paint it, tile it, or line it with a mosaic of pebbles, sea shells, or whatever you have available.

Let a pool draw attention to arrangements of container plants as seasonal blooms appear. To accent the pool itself, place a glass float or colorful bloom on the water's surface. The simplest enjoyment of all is to keep the water clear and let birds play in it.

Formal pools usually require adequate space if they are to look their best. Crowding a formal pool into a small area tends to destroy vital esthetics that depend upon proper scale. Traditionally, a formal pool may contain a piece of sculpture; such classic treatment has an old world look about it.

Informal designs, on the other hand, seem to fit comfortably in limited space. Sharply defined geometric forms are the mark of utilitarian design, showing definite urban influence. Or a pleasant looking scene, such as pictured on the left, can be installed off a patio or in a similar small area. A natural-appearing pool is the most enjoyable to create. It is also the most demanding. The physical construction is not the difficult part, however; the problem is finding a way to assemble the rocks, soil, grasses, and other material so that the pool appears to be the work of nature. With natural pools, the objective is to create a landscaped scene so natural in appearance that the pool seems to belong right where you have placed it.

Locating your pool

Finding the right location for a pool is not always a simple matter. An obvious location for your pool, it would seem, is out where everyone can enjoy it. If such a location requires that you renovate your entire yard, though, that location is obviously impractical. You might consider an area off the master bath or perhaps a corner of your lot that is now collecting weeds. If you are planning to have fish and plants in your pool, you must consider the pool's location in relation to the sun. Water lilies require a minimum of 4 to 6 hours of sun per day, and more is desirable.

When you have formulated some ideas about the kind of pool you think you'd like, sketch them out on paper. The actual building of a pool is relatively simple once you have your design clearly in mind and a visual plan to serve as a guideline. Given fair weather, you can build and cure an average size (8 by 10 feet) pool in only a few weeks. If you are planning to create a water garden in your pool, the best time to do this is in early summer.

Floating fire *and white bloom draw instant attention and comment. Here is a decorative Japanese touch—bamboo tree as background, Nipponese ceremonial bowl filled with gravel. Obtain similar effect with saucers of flaming liquid. Small bowls challenge imagination.*

Water as a decorative accent

Water in small amounts serves a decorative purpose in a garden. It is highlighted in a showy bowl, provides an excuse to fashion a large-scale mosaic piece, or sets off a prize plant effectively.

Ideas for tiny pools spring from craftsmen, from ingenious scavengers-about in attics and garages, and from some equally inspired shoppers. The simpler bowls require few special supplies beyond the basic ingredients. Only elementary tools are needed, and previous experience or special talent is not a requirement for success.

Innovative garden decorators have demonstrated that almost any container capable of holding water can—with suitable cleaning and appropriate placement—become an attractive garden pool. Add your own ideas to the following: photographer's darkroom trays, army surplus plastic lens, bonsai bowls, furnace ducts, oil drums, wine barrels, laundry tubs, horse troughs, and hot water (and other) tanks. Scout around your house (or grandmother's) for that chipped enameled dish pan, rusty wheelbarrow, or galvanized bucket; you may even find a crock still gathering dust since Prohibition days.

(Continued on page 40)

"Our instant Japanese garden" *is what the owners jestingly call this old fashioned rustic tub. The wagon wheel leaning against it suggests that it might be a western Japanese garden. Old barrels, wooden bath tubs, horse troughs—when you can find them—make excellent raw material for small garden pools; searching is half the fun.*

Cast on sand mold, *this concrete reflecting pool is easy to make and relatively easy to move around the garden (if two people do it). Bowl is painted dark blue to accent background reflections of narcissus. The dramatic effect of blue sky reflected in water and a row of showy plants is useful in many garden nooks.*

Tiny pebbles *embedded in mortar display river bottom variety of size and shape. Pool is reinforced concrete, was cast elsewhere and brought to this location. Fountain head and recirculation pump are side by side in pool. Pump purchased at hardware store is smallest commercially available. Landscape Architect: Lawrence Halprin.*

Study in textures *is emphasized in this garden scene. Smooth, quiet water reflects rough grain of driftwood. Tall driftwood log appears to have twisted away to examine the background leaves or perhaps to hear from the 5-gallon bottle member of the grouping. Pool is a metal tank end sunk in ground. Design: Lana Christensen.*

Pools **39**

Specially designed corner *for a medium-sized portable pool. Even the lighting is a special effect. Spotlight above water is aimed at plants; pool reflects light upward, double lighting tall puffs of papyrus plants. Pool also acts as focal point of patio, although somewhat balanced by plants across patio. Design: Joseph Y. Yamada.*

Small pools of this type do have limits. They are not suitable habitats for fish or water plants. Such pools work best when dramatizing a group of container plants or in a small, neatly groomed garden where they can draw attention to a subtle bloom. Properly placed, they serve nicely as miniature reflecting pools.

Handcrafted pools from concrete

Concrete, long regarded as an industrial material—good for paving sidewalks, pouring foundations, and like projects—has acquired a new reputation. Hobbyists and craftsmen have discovered its great plasticity and free-form versatility. The sudden rise to popularity of such lightweight gravels as vermiculite and haydite has also catapulted concrete into demand as a craft material.

Small pools can be made either of standard concrete, using granite gravels, or of lightweight concrete, using a lightweight gravel. Either standard or lightweight concrete will hold water, one as well as the other. For garden use, lightweight concrete has a positive feature; it resembles stone more closely than standard concrete does.

On the other hand, standard concrete will make a more smoothly finished surface with less effort. This is an advantage when pool cleaning time arrives; smooth concrete is easier to clean and to keep clean. And smooth surfaces take paint and waterproofing compounds more readily. (A finish coat over lightweight concrete will serve the purpose. The formula is: 1 part white cement to 1 part clean sand.)

Unlimited possibilities for decorative reflecting pools are suggested by simple diversity of size, form, and location in the four examples shown here. **Top left:** the Japanese influence is appreciated by gardeners everywhere. Bamboo drip tube fills bowl; water effect is re-echoed by flat pebbles. Mushroom lantern creates unmistakable Nipponese style. Tiny plants are companions to small water bowl. **Top right:** eight feet across, this pool is barely portable, can be cast in place on a sand bed edged with stakes driven tightly together in the ground. **Bottom left:** pool made of lightweight aggregate decorates the end of a long garden bench. Bowl-shaped barbecue was used as mold. Glass floats, driftwood add decorative touch. Design: Floyd Gerow. **Bottom right:** tank ends are a popular type of salvaged pool. Garden hose hidden in plants provides active play of water—spillage has adequate drain. Design: Kaye Scott.

Classical reminiscence *is prompted by this rectangular pool and balanced garden scene. Even the trees appear to be disciplined. Paradoxically, such pools as this are often made unsightly by undisciplined algae growth. A recirculating pump helps solve the problem.*

Traditional garden pools

In a Victorian garden the pool was frequently a generous circle or rectangle, slightly raised, set in the center of an area, and surrounded by spacious walks so that it could be viewed from every side. But the Victorian garden failed to survive the disappearance of a patient, pipe-smoking professional gardener with quarters above the coach house. A few gardens are still large enough to accommodate such pools, but in most cases the pool has to be set near some border if there is to be enough room for something else. If you build a pool of brick, fitted stone, or tile in a simple shape, you'll succeed in recalling the old style.

Using brick or concrete

The ruddy face of brick is a warm and familiar friend in both formal and informal gardens. A raised pool with brick walls provides a traditional home for water lilies, goldfish, and koi.

Brick serves equally well in a modern context. Brick-in-sand patios, with sunken pools, appear regularly in contemporary surroundings. One of the greatest advantages of brick is its patterned appearance. Brick can be used gracefully to proportion the pool to its environment. The regular unit lends itself to modular design ("modular" means that a specific unit is established

Some pool forms *are like classical music scores; they need to be presented in a large area, and discordant notes are unacceptable. Landscaping around formal pools is marked by precise placement of plants and trees, and by meticulous care and pruning. The pool itself rarely departs from the standard shapes dictated by tradition.*

Semi-formal pool *in a contemporary setting is surrounded by modular brick walk to harmonize with garden wall of striated desert stone. Although pool's construction is of brick, its interior is covered by two coats of waterproof sealant. Because location receives full sun, oxygenating plants (water poppy) are used to control algae.*

Serving two purposes *this brick pool's two straight edges are also mowing strips, separating lawn, plant beds. Curved edge is self reinforcing, but adequate mortar joints there are difficult to achieve. Skilled, experienced brick-laying is required, for bricks should be set precisely on first try. Architects: Osmundson/Staley.*

Pool in brick patio *is reinforced concrete; perpendicular walls were poured into forms. Rocks set in floor simulate river bottom. Patio bricks are set in sand except for overlapping edge around pool, which is set in concrete. Rocks, plant selection, and arrangement suggest riverbank area. Landscape Architect: Lawrence Halprin.*

and all elements within the design use that unit as a base; multiples of the unit create pattern variation).

But amateur bricklayers can come to grief with bricks if they use them to form the walls of a pool. Bricks are too porous to do the job unaided. Pool walls require precisely mixed and expertly applied mortar to prevent leaks. A brick wall has just too many mortar joints; water weighs 62 pounds per cubic foot and will break through a weak spot very quickly. Even a professionally built wall will require two coats of commercial waterproofing.

Some homeowners use poured concrete to form a shell and face the above-grade portion of the shell with brick. Or they mount a brick rim atop the concrete walls of a sunken pool.

Concrete blocks sometimes do the job better than brick, especially where they have already set the garden scene through use in a foundation or in a garden wall. Their greater size means fewer mortar joints per square foot of surface, and they can be faced with tile, a mosaic design, or even brick. They are easier to reinforce than brick because of their hollow cores.

Poured concrete has its evident advantages. It is the most plastic of these materials, as well as the most impermeable. Its utilitarian character can be disguised with paint, a facing of brick, tile, or mosaic. Its forms can be lined to produce special effects. For example, the outer pool wall can be given a strong light-and-shadow pattern if you link the outer form with grapestakes. This is not so advisable for an inner pool wall if the pool is to hold fish and plants; the crannies offer footholds for algae.

Concrete does have some material disadvantages. It is heavy to work with. It uses carpentered forms, which are seldom easy to manufacture. It requires considerable post-construction care; the surface has to be kept damp for at least a week to allow it to set. And concrete contains an excess of lime that has to be cured before fish or plants can live in the water. The curing process usually takes about 10 days. (Other materials have to be cured also but require less time.)

Avoiding trouble later

A few general conditions apply to the design of your pool regardless of which materials you choose.

Sunken pools need some kind of raised border to keep ground water from running into the pool during rains. In a pool without a drain, overflow can drown plants near the pool and float goldfish overboard with fatal consequences. In a pool with an overflow drain, the pool water will probably be muddied by inflowing ground water. A border of wall an inch or two above the ground will help to prevent all of these things. A gravel-filled drain all around the pool will take care of water drainage along the surrounding surface. Such a drain can be hidden under grass. It should be 8 inches wide and a foot deep.

Having a drain pipe in a pool makes for easier maintenance. Most pools need a light cleaning each spring and fall. The lack of a drain means the pool has to be siphoned or pumped empty for cleaning, so any chemicals used in the cleaning will be hard to flush from the floor of the pool. Most homeowners, looking over their individual situations, will be able to decide on the most practical solution.

Safeguarding toddlers against garden pools is not easy. One method is simply to build a raised pool; children big enough to climb up a wall can be expected to have some respect for water. Another protective device is a screen set on pegs just a few inches below the water's surface. The pegs can be cast into the walls when the pool is built.

Patio pools *have many different personalities.* **Top left:** *large patio now entertains with piano-shaped pool opening, miniature alpine plants. Landscape Architect: Jack Gibson.* **Center left:** *unplanted and unused end of patio becomes miniature lake.* **Lower left:** *container plants were attractive, but with pool added, corner is patio's focal point. Design: Walter and Florence Gerke.* **Bottom right:** *added pool enhances papyrus plants that dominate patio. Landscape Architects: Eckbo, Royston and Williams.*

Any number of moods *can be created by the kind of plants used around a pool. Here, a naturally serene setting is established by the use of weeping willow planted behind the garden pool, flanked with low juniper. Around the rim is a soft carpet of baby's tears.*

Natural pools

A natural-appearing pool is almost any body of water without square corners, perpendicular walls, or manmade edges in sight. It should have native stone and soil close around it, along with plants common to the area in which you live.

From that point forward, the variety of choices open to the designer is as wide-ranging as the designs are beautiful. Yours could be an alpine pool, a willow-shaded pond, a tiny spring at some desert oasis, or a water retreat perhaps remembered from some vacation.

Natural pools are freeform shells of reinforced concrete. Their edges are camouflaged with lush plant materials or by artful use of large and small stones.

The difficult task is not in casting the simple shell of reinforced concrete that holds the water. For most people, the challenge is in achieving a sense of scale and fitness within the confines of an urban or suburban garden. Solutions to these problems require close observation and study or the services of landscape architects.

Use boulders to frame a pool

Framing a garden pool with boulders is not an easy way to do the job, but the results can be worth all the toil. In the intermountain West, a few landscape

An exotic idea *from Japan—stone pathway across natural pond. Stepping stones rest on earth mound below water's surface. Water lilies and other aquatic plants are rooted in bottom soil. Perimeter plantings completely cover pond's edge, provide hiding and spawning places for fish. Stone lanterns are distinctly Japanese.*

Artistically blended design—*right shore of pool is western-stone terrace; bank side re-creates a woodland river scene with carefully placed natural boulders, a waterfall at left (out of picture), low growing shrubs and background trees. Stones artfully hide concrete construction of pool. Design: Nagao Sakurai.*

Puddled crater *passes for a natural crevice. Puddling is an inexpensive way to create a watertight surface. About 3 inches of clay applied to the surface appears as part of the soil. In this scene, pebbles were added to walls and bottom, perimeter rocks placed, ground cover planted, and a dwarf Japanese elm positioned for accent.*

Designed for looking—*a pool containing sword ferns and other bog plants, water lilies, and goldfish. Here, fine leaf forms and textures, rich greens, cool water all combine with small symbolic lantern to signal touch of the Japanese landscape approach. Artfully planted shoreline hides concrete construction effectively. Design: Mario Corbett.*

Clear, cool water *in sunny location is result of abundance of oxygenating plants seen below water's surface. Water lilies are unique additions in this particular pool because pool more closely resembles a western canyon lake than a lily pond. Boulders are local stone.*

architects have succeeded in developing whole gardens around native stone. But here are some problems you might come up against:

• A man needs ample space for a boulder-framed pool. Boulders fill up space quickly, and the shell of the pool itself has to be sizable to remain in scale with the stones.

• It is hard work for most men to move stones a foot in diameter. Most such pools will require the professional services of a rockery man.

• Some types of stone—mainly the shales and other striated types—can be stacked in ways that look natural. Massive stones—the granites so common in western mountains—look far less at home in stacks. For them, it is often necessary to create a mound of earth as a framework.

• Mortaring the interstices between stones, unless done with great skill, will be evident.

Rusty rocks can produce rusty water in time. The "rust" is ferrous oxide in the stone which has mixed with moist air; it will wash out in the pool when water runs over it.

If large rocks are to be placed on the floor of the shell, here is a useful trick: break granite rocks with a sledge, carry the small pieces out into the pool one by one, and reassemble the stone with cement slurry. This technique avoids moving heavy stones across the floor of the pool and the possibility of breaking the concrete floor.

Another solution to the problem of wrestling with weighty boulders is to use fibrous rock, a plastic mass covered with granite chips and molded into an amazingly accurate replica of real stone. Sold at nurseries and garden supply centers, the stones come in many sizes. They weigh less than a fifth as much as real stone.

Freeform concrete can be stacked to a slope of about 45 degrees with ordinary mix and can be made steeper with either forms or a dry mix.

If he uses a form, the builder can employ the trick of troweling the top of the wall to a 45-degree slope. This makes it easier for plants to grow over the

Free-form fish pond—do-it-yourself

Even though the foot of a hill made a natural site for this 16 by 32-foot pool, its construction required several weeks.

Gently sloping ground formed three sides of the pool. The fourth side was built—stone atop a heavy concrete footing—and then back-filled with concrete and rubble to make a gentle slope.

A level for the built-up wall was achieved with the use of a water-filled transparent plastic garden hose (when the water stands even below each upraised tip, the hose is level).

On the uphill side, a 1 by 6-inch redwood board supported by stakes served as a perimeter marker for the concrete pour.

Stakes driven into the ground in a grid pattern established a 4-inch depth for the concrete floor. These were removed one by one as the pouring progressed to them. The stakes at the uphill side were set 1 inch lower than top of rock wall.

A drainage ditch, 8 inches wide and a foot deep, encircles the grade-level parts of the pool. It carries off drainage water, avoiding overflow in the pool and muddied water.

The concrete is standard formula transit mix, sealed with a ¼-inch sealer coat of 1 part cement, 1 part sand. Commercial waterproofing in two coats.

1. Rubble backfill *strengthens wall. Floor excavated to assure general depth of 2 feet required by fish.*

2. Stakes *in grid pattern showed how deep to pour concrete. Were removed as pouring reached them.*

3. Concrete *was tamped down around grid pattern of reinforcing rods to eliminate air pockets in floor.*

4. Rocks *were broken, then reassembled with mortar in place, to avoid rolling them across floor.*

Free-form concrete *shell designed especially to hold fish. Uphill sides have trough to exclude runoff from rains, a winter problem. Summer heat causes evaporation loss of about 1 inch in depth each week. Design: William Steward.*

rim, hiding the edge of the pool. Another method is to lure plants over the edge by regularly brushing the edge of the pool with liquid fertilizer.

Special effects with bridges

Three basic bridge building materials are wood, cast concrete, and quarried stone. Wood is the commonest, most versatile, lightest, and least expensive. Bridges made entirely of cast concrete can be almost any length provided that the concrete is adequately reinforced. Quarried stone is a frequently used bridge material in Japanese-style gardens. When you use stone, it's better to build short spans with ends firmly set in a solid surface, preferably concrete.

A bridge designed for foot traffic should be 2 to 3 feet wide in order to promote a sense of security for those who may walk across it. Unless they are quite large, most wooden bridges do not need concrete footings at the ends. If the ground is solid, small structures can be attached with pegs or other material. Be sure, though, that all lumber coming in contact with the ground is treated with a chemical sealer.

Curving beams *are cut from 2 by 12-inch planks for this bridge, resting on concrete pads at each end. Oriental garden and occidental patio (out of photo at left) work nicely together. Patio is higher than pool, retains western identity. Pool is in partial shade at all times. Design: Mario Corbett.*

Bridges: complex to simple. Top left: *this bridge isn't really complex; it just seems that way because its construction requires more work than the other two. It employs old telephone poles and used lumber, serves as entryway to house.* **Top right:** *four snow-bent saplings, tied at top and bottom, hold cross pieces on arched, old style water crossing.* **Bottom left:** *simplest of all is do-it-yourself bridge that you can nail together in an hour.*

Striking colors *of Japanese koi, water lilies, bog plants dominate semi-natural pond visible from breakfast room (behind woman) in fenced entry court. Potted bonsai tree accents oriental design of the garden.*

Water Gardens and Fish Ponds

Regardless of the kind or number of plants and fish that you put in your pool, your first consideration should be the pool's ecological maintenance. Make immediate plans to deal with algae. The formation of algae in a pool is a natural thing; a certain amount of it is inevitable in any pool. But if not controlled, this tiny aquatic plant (related to seaweed) can cover the water's surface with an ugly green scum. For this reason, a "balanced pool" has practical value for the homeowner.

When water gardeners speak of a balanced pool, they're referring to its ecological balance. A balanced pool is one in which the growth of algae is controlled naturally. It is a pool in which nature does most of the work; its composition is dictated by the immediate natural environment. This means that a beautifully balanced pool in one garden could turn into unsightly chaos in another area—at least until a balance suitable to the local environment could be achieved. By patiently observing and cooperating closely with nature, you can establish a balanced pool that requires little maintenance. A pool nurtured in this manner will be rewardingly trouble free.

George L. Thomas of Lilypons, Maryland, who raised both water plants and fish professionally for several decades, recommends what he calls "green water."

"Healthy pool water," Mr. Thomas advises, "is not crystal clear but has a slightly cloudy, greenish tinge. This green cast is due to the millions of suspended microscopic algae, plankton, and similar plants which are necessary for the health of goldfish. It is easy to determine the proper balance of these plants in the pool water. Roll up your sleeve and hold your hand about 12 inches below the surface. If your hand is barely discernible at that depth, the balance is perfect."

Because environmental conditions and pool designs, together with pump and plumbing installations, are so extensively varied, no general rule for controlling algae can be stated that will apply precisely to even a large percentage of pool installations. One must either use a mechanical device that fits the individual pool design or attempt to establish a balanced pool. If you seek information from a professional source about algae control, make sure that you both agree on what constitutes an attractive garden pool. Professionals sometimes differ widely in their concepts of the algae problem and in their solutions to it.

Grab bag *of attractive, useful plants stock this pool. Sword ferns shade top side of pool. Water lily is at center, water poppy (an oxygenating plant) to right of lily. Primrose creeper is at left center. Parrot feather is at lower right.*

Plants in and around the pool

Gardening possibilities multiply instantly when you add a pool to your garden. In the pool itself you can put three kinds of plants: 1) those with roots in soil and their leaves floating on the surface—water lilies for example; 2) such floating plants as water hyacinth or water lettuce, whose roots dangle in the water; and 3) oxygenating plants, which are totally submerged. Some plants grow best around the pool's perimeter where the water splashes, keeping the ground wet; these are called bog plants.

Far outnumbering other water plants, water lilies cover an extraordinary and exotic range of color, size, and shape in both day and night blooming species. For this reason we treat them as a special feature on pages 60-61. In contrast, only a few of the floating plants—among them, water hyacinth and water lettuce—are sold at water plant nurseries in the United States. The worker plants - oxygenators - grow beneath the pool's surface. Although they do not bloom and are rarely seen, they are, nevertheless, indispensable to a balanced pool. Of the bog plants there are about 35 different kinds. Bog plants can camouflage a pool's concrete edge effectively, giving the pool a more natural appearance.

Plants in the pool

In pools that are less than 2 feet deep, it is possible to plant directly into soil at the bottom of the pool. Most water gardeners, however, like the versatility of

Dwarf umbrella plant (Cypernus haspan) *is a small member of the papyrus family. Although similar in habit and foliage to other papyrus, it is used where its taller relatives would appear out of scale. Here it grows in evenly spaced sections of terra cotta pipe. Landscape Architects: Eckbo, Royston, and Williams.*

Violet water hyacinth *grew so rapidly when introduced in Florida streams that it became a menace to navigation. Water hyacinth is a floating plant, remaining buoyant on inflated, spongy stems. Blooms are borne in clusters on erect spikes. Do not keep them with koi, for the fish shred the roots which, in turn, clog the filter.*

Sculptor's retreat *is a 7 by 15-foot water garden. The deck is his place to relax. Concrete pool contains papyrus, water lilies, water hyacinths, and goldfish. Background plants are bamboo (right), coconut palms (center). Sculptor has alternately carved two marine forms—scallop and starfish—on boards along length of redwood fence.*

Water poppy (Limnocharis humboldtii) *is a three-petaled, yellow flower resembling the California poppy. Roots are embedded in submerged soil, usually in pots. Runners rise to surface, produce new plants that send runners to pool bottom for fresh rooting. This plant is attractive if controlled, a nuisance otherwise.*

movable boxes that allow easy access to the plants. This portable feature of the planters facilitates pool cleaning and allows better plant control.

Here are a few of the water plants that do very well in a water garden:

Arrowhead (*Sagittaria graminea*). Belongs to the same genus as an arrowhead that is planted around the pool, but this one is quite different. Primarily an oxygenator, it grows freely in water with its grasslike leaves mainly submerged.

Azolla floats on the water's surface, is a fast-growing, mosslike plant and is best used in small pools where it can be controlled. In the shade its color is green, but it turns red in the sun.

Duckweed (*Lemna minor*) has tiny leaves that cover a pool very quickly. Unless given almost constant attention, this plant can be quite a nuisance. One expert notes that fish eat its tender roots which act as a laxative and serve nicely as a fish tonic.

Elodea is an oxygenator that needs a lot of sun. A perennial, it propagates by runners. Full, slender foliage grows under water. To control it, pinch off the old growth.

Lotus (*Nelumbo*) is an East Indian lotus, one of those plants that appears difficult to grow but really isn't. Thick stems rise from rootstocks in spring, supporting the magnificent round leaves above the water's surface to 5 or 6 feet. Flowers, often a foot across, are held above the leaves and are single or double in pink, or white and red combinations.

Parrot's feather (*Myriophyllum brasiliense*) has light green, feathery leaves that drift on the surface of the water. Roots provide a good spawning area for fish.

Eel grass (*Valisneria*) leaves grow long and ribbonlike as high as 2 feet. A very good oxygen plant.

Water hawthorn (*Aponogeton distachyus*) has a winter flowering habit that is unique among the common aquatics. It needs 8 inches of water for its tuberous rootstocks. Narrow leaves float on the water.

Water hyacinth (*Eichornia*) includes two species, *E. crassipes* and *E. azurea*. *E. crassipes* was introduced into Florida streams and grew so rapidly that it menaced navigation. In a garden, however, it is a valuable plant, having violet flowers with a yellow eye borne in clusters on erect spikes. The choicer species is *E. azurea*. It bears purplish blue flowers with a peacock eye in the center. It moors itself to the bottom as a water lily does.

Water lettuce (*Pistia stratiotes*), also known as shell flower, comes by its name from its appearance. It floats on the surface trailing its hairlike roots. Although it does fairly well in partial shade, it needs daily exposure to the sun. This plant seems to thrive when near a spray of some kind, perhaps a fountain. Leaves are bluish green.

Plants around the pool

Border plants thrive on the moist soil around the pool, providing a handsome backdrop for the plants in the pool. Possible bog species include the following:

Baby's tears (*Helxine soleirolii*). Creeping, mosslike, perennial herb with tiny white flowers makes cool, luxuriant ground cover near pools. Use it where it won't be stepped on, in shade.

Primrose willow (*Jussiaea repens*). A vine for pool's edge. Needs 1 inch of water or very soggy soil. Produces waxy green leaves and tall, primroselike yellow flowers.

Elephants ear (*Colocasia esculenta*). Very showy plant of medium height gives garden a tropical look. Needs shade or partial shade. Spreads by root division.

(Continued on page 58)

Horsetail plant (Equisetum hyemale) *is a perennial that enjoys extraordinary popularity among water gardeners. A rushlike plant, its origin reaches into prehistoric eras. Here it is planted in a concrete box, near an adequate water supply. A rare snip of the pruning shears and occasional feeding is all the care it needs.*

Background plantings *and landscaping efforts should be very carefully planned before any work is done. Here, a semi-natural pond is completely open to view on house side but closed off from neighbors by trees at back of property. Pond has great potential as fish pool or water garden. Recirculation pump and pebbled bottom keep water clear.*

Rustic footbridge, rich green border foliage, realistic boulder placement, *and mature trees combine in artistic scale around long, almost creeklike pond containing water plants and goldfish. Border plants are juniper, rushes, dwarf umbrella plant, sword ferns. Other water plants not shown are horsetail and tall papyrus. Trees are pine and redwood. Entire scene is entryway to house. Suburban street is just beyond tree trunk, right center at top of photograph. Driveway, behind camera, is lined with same plants as border pond. Steel and mesh reinforce concrete pond shell laid on a bed of river gravel.*

Papyrus *(Cyperus papyrus)*. Will grow to 6 to 10 feet but can be kept pruned to 5 feet. Noted for foot-long tufts of threadlike flower stalks at tops'of reedlike stems. Root in several inches of water and plant in sun.

Giant arrowhead *(Sagittaria sagittifolia)*. From dark green arrow-shaped leaves emerge spikelike clusters of white flowers. Grows 1 to 4 feet, spreads by runners. Thin occasionally.

Horsetail *(Equisetum hyemale)*. One of the most popular pool plants, this ·vigorous grower is best controlled in a container whether planted in or near the pool. Bright green jointed stems give vertical accent. Needs afternoon shade.

Plantain lily *(Hosta plantaginea)*. Large, shiny, heart-shaped leaves and white, scented flowers. Ideal at shallow edge of pool. Spreads rapidly. Propagate by root division.

Umbrella plant *(Cyperus alternifolius)*. A relative of the Egyptian paper plant, it thrives in shallow water or moist ground achieving a height of 2 feet. Propagate by division or seeds.

Water canna *(Thalia)*. Deep purple flowers on long arching stems distinguish this perennial herb. Bold, spear-shaped foliage. Flourishes in an inch or two of water.

Water iris *(Iris versicolor)*. Sought after for their color (blue purple) and their dense foliage. Blooms late spring. Needs moisture.

Water poppy *(Hydrocleys nymphoides)*. Miniature yellow flowers bloom best when plant is in 1 to 3 inches of water.

Other landscaping ideas

Bamboo is a staple in pool landscaping. It adds an often desirable vertical dimension to a garden setting. Bamboo grows quickly and likes the moist soil near the pool area. It combines handsomely with elephant ears and flowering ginger.

Bamboo will be an even more enjoyable plant if kept under control, and this is best accomplished *before* planting. Tubs, pots, boxes, or raised beds will contain rampant growth; or use an 18-inch-deep barrier of sheet metal, pressed asbestos, or poured concrete bulkhead.

Among the many types of bamboo, several do especially well in the West and are well suited to the pool garden.

Golden bamboo *(Phyllostachys aurea)*. Grows as high as 30 feet, but usually much less. Stem diameter is 2 inches. Good screen for sun control, privacy. Does well in tubs.

Yellow groove bamboo *(Phyllostachys aureosulcata)*. Very hardy runner. Hardy to 20°, a good one to try in cold areas. Grows to 30 feet with a diameter of 1½ inches.

Metake, arrow bamboo *(Pseudosasa japonica)*. Grows to 18 feet; ¾-inch diameter. Stem sheaths never fall and plant sheds little.

Low bamboo *(Sasa humilis)*. Ground cover that gets about 3 feet tall. Graceful arching stems. Rampant runner. Good in borders.

Dwarf bamboo *(Sasa pygmaea)*. Good ground cover in fairly moist areas. Aggressive spreader. Grows 1 foot tall. If carefully contained, makes nice touch near pool.

These bamboos clump, rather than spread:

Fernleaf hedge bamboo *(Bambusa multiplex* 'Fernleaf'*)*. Narrow, closely spaced leaves, 1 to 20 per twig. Loses ferny quality in rich soil. Reaches 10 to 20-foot heights. Diameter, ¼ inch.

Golden Goddess *(Bambusa multiplex* 'Golden Goddess'*)*. Similar to above but larger leaves and 8 to 10-foot height. Easy to control. Widely available.

Achieving an attractive setting *requires careful planning, keeping the background always in mind.* **Top:** *trees frame medium-size Japanese style landscape. Tidy, well placed evergreen shrubs appear compact against leafy skyline. Crane and lantern balance one another nicely with stream, boardwalk running between. Walk and fence meet at bushy tree at right.* **Bottom left:** *textures range evenly from bottom to top—translucent water blends into pebbles and solid rock that lead to leafy bower.* **Bottom right:** *Most often viewed from deck at left, this garden is designed for that perspective. Note how stream wanders off into trees from end corner of deck (by the dwarf umbrella plant). Rock placement and fertile banks imitate natural stream in this balanced, sunny area. Water contains fish, water lilies, snails, and oxygenating plants.*

All colors in the rainbow—the water lilies

Water lilies (*Nymphaea*) will almost certainly be more widely planted when more gardeners come to appreciate their beauty, dependability, and the ease with which they can be grown. Hardy water lilies bloom during daylight, opening about 10 A.M. and closing after sunset, but tropicals include both day and night-blooming varieties. Most flowers live four days, once open; they last just as long if they're cut. (To keep cut flowers open apply melted paraffin or candle wax with an eyedropper around the base of the stamens, petals, and sepals.)

Hardy water lilies can be planted from early spring through October in mild-winter areas. Although the tropicals can be grown in all areas, they shouldn't be planted until average daytime temperatures rise above 65 degrees—normally after the first of May. If set out at the recommended times water lilies begin to flower in one to four weeks. Hardy lilies flower early in April and tropicals produce their first blooms in May. The best tropicals will bear up to three times as many flowers as the hardy lilies.

How to grow them

You can grow all kinds of water lilies in a pool with vertical sides and a uniform depth of 18 to 24 inches. If the sides of the pool have a gradual slope, the water there is subject to extreme temperature variations that are unhealthy for your water plants. And, algae grows faster in the shallows.

Both hardy and tropical water lilies require full sun—4 to 6 hours each day is minimum—to open the flowers. If you have to build your pool in partial shade, choose a location that gets the morning sun.

Planting. Use a rich garden soil for planting water lilies but don't add manure, peat moss, or ground bark to the soil. It has been found that manure encourages the growth of algae and fouls the water. Peat moss and ground bark will float to the surface and cloud the water.

Mix about a pound of slow-acting, granular type fertilizer with the soil for each lily that you're planting. A complete fertilizer with a nitrogen content between 3 and 5 per cent is considered almost ideal. Most water lily growers sell a specially formulated fertilizer.

Plant only one water lily in each box so that the leaf pattern of each plant will be displayed to best advantage. The top should be covered with about an inch or more of pebbles to prevent clouding the water. The top of each box should be 8 to 12 inches below the surface of the water.

Seasonal care. Remove yellowing leaves, faded flowers, and fruits periodically. Lopping shears or pole pruners are convenient tools if you have to reach far out over the water. The foliage of established plants may lose its normal green color several years after planting; you can feed these plants by placing a fertilizer tablet in the root zone.

Aphids, the commonest pest of water lilies, can be controlled by washing the plants with a garden hose. If you have fish, they will soon consume the aphids. For heavier infestation, you can apply oil spray at growing-season strength; this will not adversely affect the fish, snails, or plants. Apply the spray on dull days or in the evening to prevent leaf scorch.

Hardy water lilies, *such as this large-flowered white one, can be planted in early spring. These lilies, the easiest for beginners to grow, are available in every color.*

Tropical water lily *called Haarstick (for its developer) is glowing red. Here, three blooms are open and two are preparing to unfold. Tropicals bloom day and night.*

Combine *2-inch-deep layer of soil (right), 1 pound slow-acting fertilizer (center). Top with 4 inches of soil.*

Holding *plant in place, add soil around roots, firming as you go. Set root crown even with rim, or just above.*

Cover *soil with 1-inch-deep layer of coarse sand or fine gravel to keep soil from dispersing and clouding water.*

You can grow all kinds *of water lilies, and most other water plants, in a pool of this size and shape—3 by 8 feet by 18 inches deep. This tile-lined pool has the advantage of 90-degree vertical sides.*

This tropical water lily *produced three blooms. A single plant may provide as many as 4 or 5 in summer.*

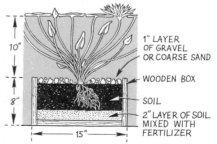

1" LAYER OF GRAVEL OR COARSE SAND

WOODEN BOX

SOIL

2" LAYER OF SOIL MIXED WITH FERTILIZER

10"

8"

15"

Cross section *of basic arrangement for water lilies planted in wooden planter box; minimum depth is 6 inches.*

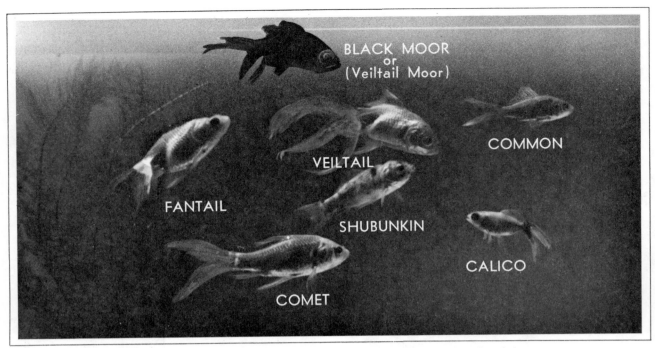

Goldfish (Carassius auratus) *are the patriarchs of ornamental fish; fancier breeds have come from them. Only the veiltail may not survive in cold-winter areas, but it is fairly durable. All of the other goldfish shown here are hardy types, commonly placed in outdoor pools.*

Keeping fish in a pool

Overfeeding, overcrowding, and shock from rapid temperature changes or rough handling are the main causes of early death among fish that are kept as pets. Nature does not overfeed or overcrowd fish when they live in a natural habitat, and almost the only time she shocks them is when it's time for spawning. Professional fish breeders suggest that homeowners attempt to simulate the natural environment as closely as possible.

Here is how it works: In their natural state, fish—like birds—are in constant search of food. They eat whenever they find something edible, but overeating is rarely a problem for them. In a garden pool, though, if the owner supplies too much food or supplies it too often, the fish may, quite literally, eat themselves to death.

When you first put fish in your pool, let them have an adjusting period to the new environment. Give them at least 24 hours to begin hunting before you put a small amount of food in the water. Fish in search of food are more active and are naturally healthier than pampered fish. When they have had enough to eat and no more is available, you may find them sinking to the bottom of the pool and staying there until they feel the need to hunt again.

Another feature of the wild kingdom is "survival of the fittest." If too many fish accumulate in a specific area, the weaker fish simply do not survive. By putting too many fish in your pool you will bring about similar consequences. You will lose some of your fish because of overcrowding.

Shock, the third element, has a double effect which is rather interesting. If you accidentally shock the entire school of fish—through a rapid change in temperature—they will begin to spawn quickly because that is the way nature signals spawning time. But if you shock an individual fish, it is likely to become sluggish, display dull fins, and become lighter in color. The fish may survive, or it may die, depending on the extent of its injury.

Shock among fish is not immediately noticeable, but eventually it weakens their resistance to disease. The most likely time for shock occurs when you transfer fish from the pet store to your pool. Don't dump the fish into a pool that you have just filled with water. Fill your pool several days before adding fish to allow the chemical components in the piped-in water to dissipate. After you pick up your fish, place the fish container outdoors for about eight hours so that the water temperature in the container will become equal to the water temperature in the pool. Then lower the container into the pool and let the fish swim out; don't dump the fish into the water.

Goldfish

Goldfish come to mind automatically at the mention of fish pools in a garden. These small members of the carp family have been bred for centuries as hobby fish; consequently there are countless varieties. These are varieties recommended for outdoor use: Common, Comet, Calico, Fantail, Moor, Shubunkin, and Veiltail.

Goldfish live comfortably in water ranging from 50 to 80 degrees but prefer the narrower range from 60 to 70 degrees. Although they can endure a winter under ice, they will eat very little and will not grow during the cold winter months. (To prevent ice formation, cover the pool with boards topped by a layer of straw.)

Balancing your pool

In a balanced pool, here is how balance is achieved: goldfish, koi, or tropical fish breathe in oxygen and expel carbon dioxide. The carbon dioxide is used by the plants which release oxygen into the water. With fish in your pool, you must supplement the water's oxygen supply with an abundance of submerged oxygenating plants. Acting in direct competition to the sunlight (on which algae thrive), these plants keep the water clear and provide spawning places for the fish. In addition to algae and the food you supply to them, fish feed on insect larvae, keeping the mosquito problem around your pool to a minimum. Snails placed in the pool will consume algae formations on the sides of the pool and on plants. But if you add too many snails, they may attack your plants.

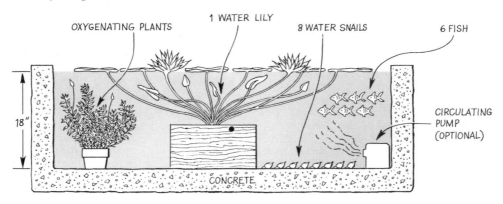

OXYGENATING PLANTS 1 WATER LILY 8 WATER SNAILS 6 FISH

CIRCULATING PUMP (OPTIONAL)

18"

CONCRETE

Koi eat from your hand, accept pats on the head

A koi pool can be any size or shape. However, depth is important—no shallower than 18 inches and ideally between 24 and 36 inches, or deeper. It also must be large enough so the fish have room to swim—at least 10 feet across. An ideal pool would be concrete with an 8-inch-thick base and 6-inch-thick walls. It would have shallow places for feeding and fish watching and deeper water where the fish can go when surface water heats up or starts to freeze—or to escape a predator like the family cat. Koi don't mind a change in water temperature if it's gradual. There's less temperature fluctuation in deeper pools.

Place the pool where it gets some shade. This is both good for the fish (colors tend to be richer and deeper in shade) and will keep down the formation of algae.

If you really want to enjoy your colorful koi, pool water should be as clear as possible. It's not that koi or carp necessarily prefer clear water; in nature they're bottom feeders in lakes and streams. But domesticated koi seem to be bothered less with pests and diseases in clear water. One reason is that you can spot a problem before it gets out of hand. Water filters will keep pool water clear. But we've seen pools that are absolutely crystal clear and have no filters. Water is simply circulated so that fouled water is naturally forced up a pipe from the bottom and flows out a spillway.

Herb Simon, koi importer and pool builder in Hayward, California, uses a biological filter system. A layer of coarse, aquarium-type gravel at the bottom of the pool contains bacteria that eliminate all fish waste matter. A 1-horsepower pump recirculates the water over a waterfall. A small amount of fresh water is pumped into the system constantly, and an equal amount of "aged" water is drained out of the pool. This is accomplished by attaching a water flow control valve to the water tap; the aged water drains out through the overflow pipe. For pools containing up to 500 gallons, a 1/8 gpm (gallons per minute) control valve is used—up to 2000 gallons, a 1/2 gpm valve,—and, up to 4000 gallons, a 1 gpm valve. This filtration system never needs cleaning. In full sun, on which algae growth thrives, the gallons per minute recirculation rate is simply increased, and the koi eat the small amount of algae that does form on the pool walls.

Commercial "high-rate" sand filters are available in capacities ranging from 200 to 400 pounds of sand. They are called high rate because water is pumped through the sand at a rate of 50 to 100 gpm. The containers are made of either stainless steel or fiberglass; it is easier to change the sand with the stainless steel model. These commercial types are either semi-automatic or fully automatic. The difference between them is that the semi-automatic requires your presence for two minutes each day to backwash the sand, whereas the fully automatic filter contains a pressure sensing device that backwashes as the sand requires it.

Koi clubs

If there is a koi club in your area, you might join it. More knowledgeable members will help you in your purchases and recommend the best dealers. You'll also learn about pests and diseases and how to prevent or cure them.

Koi clubs sponsor shows where you'll be able to learn what makes a show winner and which fish are considered best in their class. For a list of western koi clubs, koi dealers, and public displays of koi, send a stamped, addressed return envelope to Koi Editor, *Sunset Books*, Menlo Park, Calif. 94025.

Japanese koi (Cyprinus carpio) *are carp, not goldfish. They're sometimes called samurai or warrior fish, not because they're belligerent or fight among themselves but because they are determined swimmers, able to negotiate rapids, ascend waterfalls. Breeders name them for their colors.*

Family pets, *koi, come when called, follow owners around the pool, take food from outstretched fingers, and will allow themselves to be petted. Koi outlive almost any other kind of pet, may even outlive their owners. The word koi is Japanese; in America koi are known as carp.*

Daily at 3 P.M., *132 koi in this pool gather for supper. Koi eat both animal and vegetable foods. Pet shops sell prepared koi food that you can supplement with shrimp, crab, worms, lettuce, cabbage, carrots, watercress, cooked egg. Overfeeding fouls water as food decomposes.*

Koi are given Japanese names *for their colors: one-color are white, Shiro-muji; red, Aka-muji; yellow, Ki-goi; gold, Ohgon; orange, Orange-ohgon; and platinum, Shiro-ohgon. Two colors; red on white, Kohaku; black on white, Shiro-bekko; white on black, Shiro-utsuri.*

Koi pool is protected *from cats, raccoons, and other small animals by battery-charged, low voltage shock-wire that discourages predators. Pets and other small animals can do very expensive damage to a koi pool. Other protection includes raised borders, screens, and fencing in the pool.*

Building and Maintaining Your Pool

A garden pool or fountain can call for a wide variety of skills on the part of its builder, who may have to wear the hats of carpenter, mason, plumber, tile-setter, electrician, and painter before he is done.

Even if he must serve a stint in each of these roles, a weekend home handyman should find himself equal to the tasks, because the pools or fountains that fit into home gardens would in most cases make good first exercises for new apprentices at each of these trades. Single purpose and small scale keep confusion to a minimum. No step need be hurried.

The following pages in this chapter deal with the nuts-and-bolts problems of design and construction, one by one, before reaching the subject of maintenance.

The matter of masonry

The great majority of garden pools and fountains are made of concrete, or concrete in combination with bricks, concrete blocks, or natural stone.

Appearance, cost, and other non-structural factors govern many choices of one material over another for pool walls. For pool floors, concrete is more often used because of the structural consideration that it is far less likely to develop leaks than brick or other fitted-piece floors having numerous mortar joints.

Working with concrete

Concrete has a number of advantages over other materials used in pool construction. It is strong, can be cast in any shape, and can be reinforced with a minimum of fuss. It can be finished smoothly to minimize the difficulties of painting, water-sealing, or algae control. Concrete can be faced with tile, pebble, or glass mosaics to disguise utilitarian appearance.

On the debit side, concrete in volume requires a program for pouring in order to avoid weak joints. It can be very heavy to work with. Except in cases where it is being poured as a shell in a shallow depression, concrete requires well-carpentered forms to make walls. Finally, concrete can be difficult to patch if cracks should appear sometime after the pool's completion.

Formula. The old standard—1 part cement, 2 parts sand, 3 parts coarse aggregate —serves best in most cases. Coarser mixes do not produce the kind of watertight face that is desirable in a pool.

Experts recommend that 5 gallons of water be added to each "one-sack batch" of mix (1 sack of cement, 2 cu. ft. of sand, 3 cu. ft. of coarse aggregate). This assumes damp sand. An extra half-gallon of water with dry sand or a half-gallon less with wet sand will produce a medium-stiff consistency. The mix should be stiff enough so that it will flow very slowly after being mounded with a shovel. Wall mixes are stiffer than floor mixes.

Sand should be kept free of any vegetable matter (leaves, wood chips) or loamy earth to avoid weak spots in floor or walls. Coarse aggregate should be no larger than 1½-inch sand-free mesh for the same reason.

Estimating amounts. Mixed in small batches, concrete will finally produce about two-thirds the volume of its dry parts. This occurs because adding water compacts the dry mix by about a third.

Five sacks of cement, 10 cu. ft. of sand, and 15 cu. ft. of aggregate will make about 20 cu. ft. of concrete.

A pool 6 feet long, 3 feet wide, and 18 inches deep will require about that much concrete if floor and walls are uniformly 4 inches thick (allowing for a small amount of waste).

Mixing. The best solution for a larger-sized pool is the rental of a half-bag cement mixing machine. The powered variety makes relatively light work of this never-easy task. Amounts of only a few cubic feet can be mixed with a shovel on a board.

With the half-bag mixer, get ready half a sack of cement, 1 cu. foot of sand, and 1½ cu. feet of aggregate. Draw 2½ gallons of water in a bucket (mark it beforehand with daubs of paint).

Toss cement and sand into the mixer; let them blend until no streaks of brown or gray remain. Add the aggregate and let turn until the pebbles are uniformly coated with the dust. Then pour the water in and let the mix turn for three minutes or until no dry spots remain.

Tip the mix into the forms or into a wheelbarrow.

Hand-mixing on a board makes for a longer day, but for small amounts it is a practical method. The main requirements are a sheet of plywood, two shovels, and a marked water bucket. The plywood should be free of holes to prevent water and cement from leaking through, weakening the mix.

One shovel is for mixing dry materials; the other is used to stir the wet mix.

Heap the mixings on the board a shovelful at a time, keeping in line with the overall proportions. When the ingredients are blended, form the mix into a volcano and pour water into the cone. Use three quarts of water for each shovelful of cement in the batch. Scoop dry mix from the inside of the cone into the water, taking care not to break the dam.

On the first try, it does not hurt to add water sparingly until the mix reaches a point where its final consistency appears to be too stiff. This will avoid producing too sloppy a batch.

Forms and pouring. In designing and building the forms for a garden pool, the idea is to come up with something that will produce a unified shell through one, continuous pour.

For a free-form pool, the forms may be nothing more than stakes to indicate the depth of the pour. For a more formal effort, the carpentry will be more extensive. In either case, reinforcing rods or wire need the builder's close attention if he is to avoid cracks in the pool later.

For a standard, rectangular pool, there are two approaches. The above-grade pool uses the same forms used for any wall. A below-grade pool's forms might be simplified by omitting the outer form if the soil is firm enough to stand without crumbling.

When full forms are used, the inner wall form should end at the finished depth of the floor. In most cases, builders suspend the inner wall from cross pieces of 2 by 4s nailed securely to the outer wall form supports. The inner wall forms merely hang until the floor is poured. Then, 2 by 4 or other scrap lumber pieces are set across each dimension of the pool and nailed to brace the inner form before the walls are poured. Nail short diagonal braces into corners for added insurance. (See drawings below.)

These general considerations apply to reinforcing, forms, and pouring techniques:

1) Any form should be coated with light oil, preferably a clean or fairly clean auto crankcase oil. This will keep the forms from sticking.

2) Use a flat-bladed shovel or some other tool to jog concrete inside the face of the form. This works gravel back from the face, making the wall smoother and more waterproof.

3) If walls are at right angles to the floor, take great pains to tamp the first layer of the wall pour thoroughly. Failure to do this may leave weakening pockets of air at corners, an invitation to later cracks and leakage.

4) For sunken pools, provide at least an inch of lip above grade level if muddy rainwater is not to flow into the pool with each storm. This is a special concern if the pool has no drainage system since overflows are a potential hazard.

In the cases of natural pools, gravel-filled drain ditches around the circumference of the pool can

Molds and forms for concrete

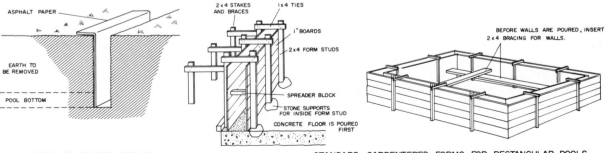

SIMPLEST FORM FOR PORTABLE BOWLS

EDGE FORM FOR LARGE BOWL — OR NATURAL POOL

HOW TO GET A SLOPING FORM

EASY FORM FOR SUNKEN POOLS

STANDARD CARPENTERED FORMS FOR RECTANGULAR POOLS

solve the problem without disturbing the appearance of the shoreline. Typically, these should be 8 inches wide and 12 inches deep.

5) Before pouring begins, set up the cross-grid of reinforcing rods so that they are all about 2 inches from the soil. In the floor, the rods can be set up on stones, chunks of brick, or any other handy piece of rubble. For walls, simply drive the rods into the earth.

Through the course of the pour, check and re-check each section to make sure that concrete is worked down through the rods and to make sure that the rods do not slip up or down from the desired level.

6) In pouring the walls, keep the pour progressing evenly all the way around the pool. Don't try to bring one section to full height before moving on to the next.

7) In excavating, make the ground slope toward the drain rather than providing for drainage at pouring time by decreasing the thickness of the floor. Two inches is plenty of slope.

Using lightweight concrete

Sometimes, plans call for "lightweight" concrete. Most of these are for small decorative projects which do not involve masses of concrete.

The term "lightweight" refers to the special use of porous gravels in place of the usual granite. Porous material is especially adapted to portable bowls and the like. It does not have enough strength for massive products and is not at its best as a sunken shell.

Vermiculite is the lightest of these porous aggregates. Haydite is both heavier and stronger. Two others that are frequently used are pumice and perlite.

Formula. These vary with use. The lightest and weakest acceptable formula for vermiculite is 1 part cement and 5 parts aggregate with no sand at all. A more usual ratio is 1 · 2 (sand) · 3.

For haydite or pumice, a general formula is 1 · 2 · 3; for a very strong mix, 4 · 1 · 2.

Any lightweight concrete project should have metal reinforcing. Small-diameter bowls need no more than ¼-inch mesh metal screen. Wide, shallow bowls generally require a combination of ¼ or ½-inch rods and metal screen with the elements wired together.

Estimating volume. Lightweight concretes are rather less reliable than ordinary concrete. The best rule of thumb is to use double volume of dry parts; the addition of water compacts the mix by between a third and a half.

Mixing. A man about to crank out a lifetime supply of small bowls might use a cement mixer, but for many projects a mixing board will do nicely.

The technique is exactly like that described for regular concrete, whichever method is used.

Forms and pouring. Because there is relatively little need for structural strength in the pools and fountains made with lightweight concrete, it can be handled in all manner of whimsical ways. A number of methods are outlined briefly in the above panel of forms and molds.

These general conditions apply:

1) Shovel wet mix into the form quickly and spread it with as few trowel strokes as possible. The more the mix is worked, the greater chance it has of sagging and cracking as it dries.

2) When reinforcing, pour one layer half the thickness of the finished product. Then embed reinforcing rods or metal screen, taking care that metal does not extend into the outmost half inch of the perimeter. Finish the pour, guarding against any sudden movement that would cause the reinforcing metal to stick up through the surface.

3) Mix all the dry ingredients well before adding any water; then add the water slowly. The mix should always have a stiff consistency.

Curing and painting pools

Curing is necessary for a pool that is to support fish or plant life. Painting is necessary only for pools which need to be some color other than their natural color to satisfy the wishes of their owners.

What is curing?

"Curing" is the process of ridding new concrete of its supply of free lime, which is toxic to fish and plant life. The process —a simple one—can be left to nature if the pool owner is in no hurry.

The accepted method is to fill the new pool with water and let it sit for 24 hours. Drain, refill, and repeat three or four times. The last time, let the water stand for a week. Then rinse the pool thoroughly. Refill it and let tap water stand for 24 hours so any chemicals can dissipate. Then the pool will be safe for fish or plants.

Chemical solutions are marketed to speed this process and get the job done more quickly.

Brick pools, and concrete pools which are to retain their natural color should be given two coats of a commercial waterproofing compound in cases where a sealing coat of 1 part cement, 1 part sand is not applied or a mosaic is not used. The pool should be etched with muriatic acid (see next page) before a waterproofing compound is applied.

Painting

There are several approaches to painting a pool. Metal tanks are best painted with an asphalt emulsion since it resists rust well and adheres tenaciously to smooth surfaces. Paint of any kind may not be a sufficient protection for fish; new sheet metal cannot be sealed sufficiently to keep toxic elements out of the water. (Well-weathered metal is neutral enough to support fish, so much-used laundry tubs are safe.)

Two kinds of paint can be used on fresh concrete with success, provided the surface is prepared: masonry latex and epoxy. (If the pool is to contain fish, curing is advisable even if the pool is to be painted as well.)

Latex should be applied with a brush or roller to a clean surface. Epoxy should be applied with a brush to a spotless surface. With epoxy, the key is preparation. One dealer says, "A flawlessly prepared surface will hold a coat of paint that will last for 10 years. It becomes almost an organic part of the concrete. A carelessly prepared surface will hold a coat that may last only as many as 90 days."

Epoxy is much easier to apply on smooth surfaces than rough ones, mainly because the smooth surfaces are easier to clean thoroughly. Then, too, the paint's two elements harden quickly once mixed (2 hours is the limit); brush work goes faster on smooth concrete than on rough.

The basic steps in preparing are the same for both types of paint. While the new concrete is still damp (but fully set), etch it with muriatic acid, obtainable from hardware and paint stores. Mix 1 part acid to 2 parts tap water in a bucket of enamelware, wood, stone, or plastic—never in metal. A gallon of diluted acid will etch from 300 to 500 square feet of surface. Wearing galoshes, protective goggles (or glasses), and rubber gloves, use a long-handled brush to slosh the acid onto all surfaces. Scrub until the acid ceases to bubble and the concrete attains a uniform, open-grained texture similar to that of fine sandpaper. Wash the acid off and flush it thoroughly out of the pool (this is especially important to the man using epoxy). Note: avoid flushing the acid into the root zones of plants. It will cause temporary burns to lawn and all roots of plants.

Paint is then brushed on, usually in two or three coats, according to its manufacturer's instructions.

When repainting a pool, all traces of old paint must be removed, unless the owner put that paint there himself and plans to use the same type again. After the old coat is removed, the surface must be etched as described above or the solvents in the new paint will soften the old coat and prevent a good bond.

Pumps and plumbing in pools

Plumbing and pumps for garden pools have been improved and simplified to the point where a weekend handyman can install them himself. A homeowner too busy to do the work can have a pump installed at a comparatively modest cost. And, maintenance requirements are minor once the pool is finished and the pump is working.

The pump

The mechanical heart of a fountain or waterfall, the pump is merely a set of whirling blades through which the water passes and by which it is pressured into further motion. Motors are included with all pumps designed specifically for garden pools.

The greatest advantage of a pump over an ever-changing supply of tap water is that the same water is used over and over, which permits the growing of fish and plants and at the same time aerates the water so that it stays fresh. (Most municipal water supplies contain chemicals that do not allow the growth of tiny organisms essential to fish and plants.)

Submersible units. Fully submersible pumps range from tiny 1/55 horsepower models, which move 135 gallons of water an hour to a height of two feet, up to a husky unit which will lift 675 gallons of water an hour to a height of 12 feet.

These pumps simplify plumbing to the extreme. They sit on the floor of the pool and are hidden only by the water itself. Flexible tubing carries water to the fountain head or to the source of a waterfall. Fill and drain piping, if any, are separate. Some manufacturers market kits which include a sheet of heavy-gauge polyethylene plastic. These sheets can be spread in a shallow depression and covered with a thin layer of sand to make a temporary pool.

Aluminum Pump Performance Chart

Vertical lift in feet	Gallons per hour				
	1 foot	3 feet	5 feet	9 feet	12 feet
Pump No. 1	170	140	...	...	...
2	200	160	120	...	...
3	200	160	120	...	...
4	280	200	140	80	...
5	280	200	140	80	...
6	320	260	200	140	...
7	320	260	200	140	...
8	430	370	300	250	200

Brass & Stainless Steel Pump Performance Chart

Vertical lift in feet	Gallons per hour				
	1 foot	3 feet	5 feet	9 feet	12 feet
Pump No. 1	200	160	120	...	...
2	320	260	200	140	...
3	580	485	390	320	260
4	900	720	620	425	390
5	1200	980	840	660	540

The motors of submersible pumps are housed in watertight domes, permanently sealed, and contain a lubricating medium. They operate silently, one advantage over other types.

Other types. Other pumps, with the motors exposed to operate in the usual fashion, are available in either horizontal or vertical models. As their descriptive names indicate, one type pulls water along a level pipe from pool to pump and then pushes it upward. The other type sucks water up directly and keeps it going in the same direction. Pool designers do not recommend them. The horizontal type, which can be placed anywhere outside a pool, is frequently the answer when water has a long distance to go from pump to outlet, as is often the case with waterfalls or artificial streams.

For especially large tasks, industrial sump pumps or swimming pool filter pumps can be substituted for the more usually used models.

Don't be misled by the low horsepower ratings of pumps. A one horsepower motor can lift about 350 pounds (45 gallons) of water at the rate of one foot per second. It could move a small lake in a short time and is much larger than needed for the average garden pool.

It is often useful to get a pump that delivers a little more water than the situation demands. The flow of water can always be reduced by means of a jet, clamp, or pinched tip on the outlet pipe.

Some pumps are self-priming, but many are not and need to be installed in a flooded position (below water level) to retain their prime. Before their first use, some self-priming pumps need to be primed by forcing water from a garden hose into the pump chamber. Be sure to understand the manufacturer's directions before starting the pump, since running one dry can cause the motor to overheat and be damaged.

The electrical connection for a small recirculating pump can be as simple as plugging its waterproof cord into an existing outdoor outlet in the garden. The addition of indoor switches or other refinements usually require professional help.

The 1/50 horsepower motor takes about 15 watts of electricity, the 1/3 horsepower about 270 watts. Most pumps advertised as suitable for garden pools use about 50 to 100 watts, so the pump itself can usually be added to an existing circuit without any fear of overloading it.

For the greatest efficiency, the pump should be installed to keep the distance it has to move the water as short as possible. The non-submersible types can be concealed with shrubbery, masonry, or carpentry as the overall design permits. (Be sure to allow some way to reach it for servicing.)

The reasons for short-distance pumping are simple enough. If the pump moves a gallon of water one foot and that gallon is still in the pipe, then the next gallon to enter the pipe has to push its predecessor along, too. The more water still fighting back, the harder the pump has to work.

In using a horizontal pump, the designer might take into account the fact that these pumps *push* water up more efficiently than they *pull* it up.

Plumbing

Pipes and fittings for garden pool pumps should be of galvanized iron, brass, or plastic. Brass fittings can be used with galvanized iron pipe to make assembly and disassembly easier. On a very small pump, rubber tubing can be substituted for any pipe.

Pipe should be at least as large as the fitting on the pump calls for since smaller pipe only increases the friction between itself and the water passing through. Where no jet effect is intended, a slightly larger pipe can increase the amount of water the pump will move.

The intake pipe leading from pool to a horizontal pump should have its open end about half way (or deeper) between the bottom of the pool and the top of the water to avoid a whirlpool effect. The intake should not be close to sediment.

An elbow on the mouth facing down will stop the whirlpool effect if the intake cannot be placed deep enough otherwise. In a very shallow pool with the intake in the floor, a shell placed over the mouth of the intake will stop the whirlpool effect.

If the water is to go through a spray head, intake pipe openings should be screened with fine copper to keep the spray head from plugging. Coarser screens will do for waterfalls. (This amount of copper should not hurt fish.) Fully submersible and vertical pumps usually come with a screen built into their intakes.

Non-submersible pumps mounted out of the water can be sound-insulated by inserting a rubber mat or lengths of rubber hose between the mounting plate of the pump and the block on which it rests. To avoid potentially noisy rattle between intake pipe and pump, use a short length of radiator hose secured with hose clamps as a bridge between pipe and pump.

Following are some typical plumbing designs for a range of pools from a tiny portable one to a full-fledged stream with torrential waterfall.

Plumbing systems. A portable fountain, such as the one shown in sketch "A" on the next page, is pumped by a quiet 1/55 horsepower submersible pump. The pump is bolted to the bottom of a shallow pan of glass fiber-reinforced plastic and has a short inlet that extends up through a hole cut in the pan. It simply draws water down and then returns it through a short hose. The little pump moves water efficiently when so little lift and such short piping are involved.

Pump and plumbing systems for pools and fountains

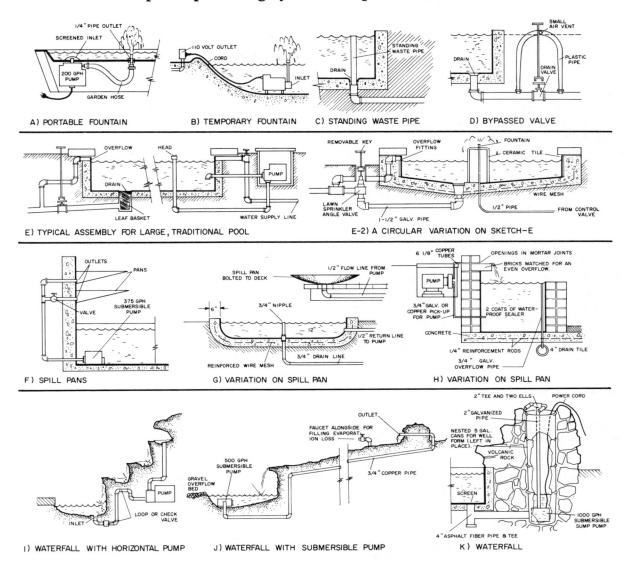

A) PORTABLE FOUNTAIN

B) TEMPORARY FOUNTAIN

C) STANDING WASTE PIPE

D) BYPASSED VALVE

E) TYPICAL ASSEMBLY FOR LARGE, TRADITIONAL POOL

E-2) A CIRCULAR VARIATION ON SKETCH-E

F) SPILL PANS

G) VARIATION ON SPILL PAN

H) VARIATION ON SPILL PAN

I) WATERFALL WITH HORIZONTAL PUMP

J) WATERFALL WITH SUBMERSIBLE PUMP

K) WATERFALL

To drain and clean such a pool, tip the pan up to dump out the water. If the pool is indoors, slip a short length of hose over the fountain head and pump the water into a pail.

A large garden pool requires considerably more plumbing to operate properly with low maintenance. Cross-section sketch "B" (see above) shows a typical design. Here again, though, the plumbing is not complex and the water pressures involved are low (it is possible to use plastic tubing).

The pump for this type of pool is usually housed below ground in a tight box. Placed lower than the water level of the pool, the pump never loses its prime. If the pump is large with an open motor (common for large pools), the underground location also helps to muffle the noise. For any open motor, the pump box should be roomy and have holes in the lid for ventilation.

The pool's drain system includes an overflow drain to prevent rain water from flooding the pool. The supply line enters above the water so the splashing is a reminder that it is turned on. For a pool of moderate size, eliminate the water supply line and fill with a hose, but a large pool takes a surprising length of time to fill this way.

Details of two other drain-overflow systems for garden pools are widely usable. These systems require only one outlet in the pool. Any overflow pours into the top of the standing waste pipe system (see sketch "C" above). To drain the pool, simply lift out the pipe. Brass pipes made for this use have a tapered end and a coupling to match; threaded pipe is used, too. Unless it can be hidden by plants or rocks, the standing pipe is quite obtrusive in the pool since it must be within easy reach.

With the bypassed valve system (see sketch "D" on page 71), open the valve (located anywhere nearby) to drain the pool. With the valve closed, any excess water escapes over the loop of plastic pipe. Raise or lower this loop to adjust the height of the pool water.

Drain lines can lead to a sewer, to a dry well or sump, or, if the water is not treated with chlorine or an algaecide, simply out onto the lawn or garden. The pool outlet needs a screen or a basket trap. If the pool is apt to gather many leaves, the drain pipe should be large (3 or 4 inches in diameter) to reduce clogging.

To use the drain water on lawn or plants located at a higher level than the pool, install a two-way valve with a hose connection on the output side of the fountain pump, install its inlet at the lowest point in the pool, and drain by pumping the water out through a hose. This eliminates the main drain entirely, though the pool will still need a small overflow drain. Normally, though, one of the drain systems shown is less bothersome, drains faster, and avoids the risk of fouling the pump with debris.

Pipefitter's primer

The addition of a pool, fountain, or waterfall to a garden often entails—as a matter of necessity or of convenience—the addition or extension of a cold water line.

Pipe-fitting *can be confined to these simple tools if you purchase prethreaded pipe for your plumbing project.*

A few simple tools, one or more lengths of standard galvanized iron pipe, some fittings, and a slight knowledge of plumbing are all the average homeowner needs to accomplish this relatively simple job.

If the pipe is bought cut to length and prethreaded, ready for assembly, these are the tools and materials needed:
• Two pipe wrenches. One should be at least a 14-inch wrench. The other should be either a 12-inch or a 14-inch wrench.
• A pair of wooden yardsticks or a 6-foot folding rule.
• Pipe compound for waterproofing joints, and a stiff brush for applying the compound.

Pipes and fittings. Galvanized iron pipe comes in a variety of sizes, indicated by the inside dimension. Most home jobs call for ¾-inch pipe (which has an outside dimension of 1-1/16 inches). However, if a ¾-inch line is already in the garden, a smaller ½-inch line leading from it may be enough for the pool or fountain.

Pipe fittings are used to join sections of pipe, to change the direction in which a pipe runs, to reduce or expand the pipe so that it can be joined to a different size pipe, or to plug the end of a pipe. The photographs on the next page show the commonest of these fittings.

Planning the installation. In adding a line or in extending one, keep the number of fittings to a minimum. The fewer number of fittings, the fewer opportunities for leaks. To use a minimum amount of pipe, it is necessary only to keep the first lesson of high school geometry in mind: a straight line is the shortest distance connecting two points.

Assembling the pipe. With an old toothbrush, first brush out the threads of both pipe and fittings, inspecting them for damage or dirt.

Next, brush on a light coat of pipe compound to all outside threads, working it into the bottom of each thread groove. Apply pipe compound *only* to outside threads, never on the threads inside fittings.

Screw joints together by hand as far as they will go. Then, slowly and gently, tighten the joints with a wrench.

Too much force with the wrenches may strip off pipe threads in the fittings. On a good joint, one or two threads will usually show. (In joining unions, a large flat wrench works better than a pipe wrench. Both faces of the union should meet squarely.)

When joints are tight, wipe off excess compound, turn on the water, and inspect for leaks. A little further tightening may be necessary. If a leak is persistent, it may be stopped by wrapping

Pipes and fittings

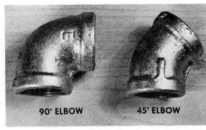

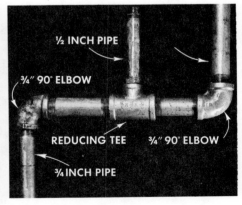

Common pipe fittings *are shown in these photos.* **Top left:** *the union is used to join pipes separated by short gap.* **Top middle:** *tees allow pipe to tap into line (reducing tee allows small pipe into larger line).* **Top right:** *bushing joins pipe and fitting of unequal sizes while reducer joins pipes of unequal size.* **Lower left:** *plug and cap are two devices for sealing ends of lines.* **Lower middle** *photo is of several lengths of nipples which are used to change direction in combination with elbows, shown at* **lower right.** *Coupling is another device to join pipe sections.*

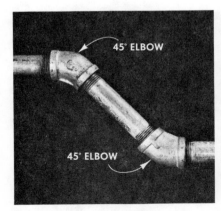

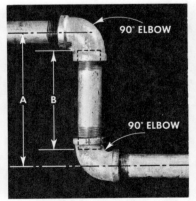

Left. *Two 45-degree elbows will produce a 45-degree jog in direction of pipe, sometimes useful for skirting obstructions.* **Middle.** *For right angle turns, subtract ¾ inch from desired length of pipe for each elbow used in pipe assembly.* **Right.** *If pool requires smaller line only, a reducing tee is used to tap off regular garden line.*

a strip of tinfoil around the joint where the pipe joins the fitting and tapping the tinfoil lightly into the joint with a hammer and screwdriver.

Plastic pipe. In some instances, plastic pipe may serve in place of the traditional galvanized iron variety. It is quicker and easier to work with and can be bent to get around corners; it is also less expensive than iron pipe. On the negative side, it is less durable than iron pipe. Burrowing rodents sometimes will take a notion to chew on it.

If plastic pipe is the solution, choose a high quality polyvinyl chloride (P.V.C.) pipe or the equivalent. Never exceed the pressures recommended by the manufacturer.

Plastic pipe fittings can be joined directly to threaded pipe. Plastic pipe can be joined to galvanized iron fittings with the aid of adapters and small clamps.

The usual procedure for extending a cold water line to a new hose bib with plastic pipe is described in the series of photographs below.

What kind of water supply?

One factor in deciding what kind of water supply a new pool should have is the rate of flow a water system will deliver, which determines the amount of time required to fill a pool.

A gallon equals 231 cubic inches. There are 1,728 cubic inches in a cubic foot, so for each cubic foot of pool there will be 7½ gallons of water.

Take into account the differences in water load capacity of the three standard-size garden hoses:

1) A ⅜-inch hose delivers from 6 to 7 gallons of water per minute.

2) The common ⅝-inch garden hose delivers from 13 to 14 gallons per minute.

3) A ¾-inch hose—the largest commonly sold—delivers about 20 gallons per minute.

Note: a pool 6 feet long, 4 feet wide, and 2 feet deep (48 cubic feet) can contain 359 gallons of water. If it were filled through a ⅝-inch hose, the process would take 25 to 35 minutes. Using a ¾-inch hose would trim the time to about 18 minutes.

Working with brick

Brick will not bend to so many whims as concrete will. Any pool wall with as many mortar joints in it as brick requires will almost certainly develop at least one leak. Brick is particularly susceptible to cracking in cold winter areas. It is harder to make waterproof than concrete and tends to collect algae more readily because of its rough surfaces.

But for all these disadvantages, brick will never disappear from the garden because of its great advantages of warm color, inherent pattern, and traditional style. No adequate substitute for those qualities will ever exist in the minds of many garden owners.

Using plastic pipe

Installing *plastic pipe involves these steps:* **1.** *T-fitting added to existing plumbing supplies plastic pipe through plastic adapter. Pipe leads to new hose bib.* **2.** *Faucet replaced on existing outlet. Plastic pipe to new bib covered by boards to protect from damage by tools.* **3.** *Metal clamp holds pipe to plastic L attached to 15-inch galvanized standpipe and faucet at site of new bib.* **4.** *Well-anchored stake supports new standpipe with two metal straps. Final step is to backfill trench. NOTE: Plastic pipe is prohibited by some municipal codes.*

A careful workman can make a sound wall of brick—one that will hold water in a pool for years. It takes excellently made mortar applied with precision and two coats of a good commercial waterseal to make a watertight wall.

A brick wall should be at least 8 inches thick—the length of one brick. There are two ways to go about building it: the wall can be two parallel rows of stretchers (bricks used lengthwise), or it can be some combination of stretchers and headers (bricks used sideways). The former method makes vertical reinforcing easier to manage since the rods can be mortared between the rows without disturbing any set pattern.

One way to simplify the problems of brick masonry is to make a thin concrete shell—three or four inches thick—and use it as the watertight interior face. A veneer of bricks on the outer face produces the desired appearance without needing to be leakproof.

Types of bricks. Bricks come in a wide range of colors and textures and a narrower range of sizes.

The standard brick measures 2½ by 3¾ by 8 inches. It is the optimum size for a one-hand lift, repeated 800 to 1,000 times a day. (This is the professional standard; a novice may find his arm gone rubbery a bit ahead of schedule.)

You can use any size or color brick for pool construction, but you should give special consideration to brick *texture*. Of the many textures of compositions marketed, the non-porous faces of pavers and standard pressed bricks are more functional than the porous surfaces of wire-cut or similar bricks. This is so because the solid surfaces take water-sealing compounds with greater grace and resist algae somewhat better.

Estimating numbers. There is no absolute way to estimate the number of bricks a pool will require because there are innumerable bonds, each of which will call for a different number of bricks.

The usual method is to decide on a bond and then work out arithmetically the number of bricks needed to make a section of the wall 2 feet long. Multiply that figure by the total number of similar units in the project and the resulting figure should be fairly accurate. In buying bricks, always get spares to cover losses through breakage or other causes. It is almost impossible to match colors between two different batches, even if both were manufactured by the same firm.

Mortar. Mortar is a mixture of cement, fine sand, and water, with a small amount of lime or lime putty added for plasticity. Proportions are 1 part Portland cement, ½ part hydrated lime or lime putty, and 4½ parts graded sand.

Sand should be "sharp," made up of angular particles, free of dirt. When wet, it should not produce a slimy deposit in the hand when it is squeezed; neither should the sand bind together. Special mortar mixes are sold at some dealers; others use a 50/50 mix of fine concrete sand and plaster sand.

Too much sand makes the mortar short. It will not hang evenly to trowel or brick; smoothly tooled joints are hard to achieve.

Almost any flat surface can be used for mixing mortar; a 2 by 2-foot square of plywood is as serviceable as any other sort. The following amounts are sufficient for 50 bricks: 1 shovelful of cement, 4½ shovelfuls of sand, ½ shovelful of lime. Mix the ingredients thoroughly in their dry state with a hoe. Scoop out a hollow, add water, and mix carefully. Continue blending and adding water until mortar slips cleanly off the blade of hoe.

Never mix more than can be used in an hour. If the batch begins to stiffen towards the end, it can be freshened with a small amount of water.

Laying brick. Only a few tools are needed for simple bricklaying. These are a 10-inch trowel with pointed blade (for buttering mortar), a brick set (a cold chisel for cutting bricks), a hammer, a two-foot spirit level, a carpenter's square, and a stretch of fishing line.

Common bricks should be damp but not wet when they are laid. If too wet, they dilute the mortar and cause it to run, and they slip in the mortar bed. The stack should be soaked with a fine spray for about an hour and a half, starting at least four hours before the laying up is to begin.

Before starting to mortar bricks in place, string out the first course dry on the pool floor. This is a last check to insure the wall's ending at the same time the floor does. Leave ½-inch spaces for mortar joints.

A professional places a stack of bricks ahead of his finished work on the wall and puts the mortar board behind him to the right. He reaches out with his trowel hand, scoops mortar onto the foundation (and each preceding course to the one he is laying) to a distance of three or four bricks. With the trowel he furrows the mortar to push it out even with the edges of the bricks. Then with his other hand, he picks up a brick and butters one end with mortar. (Most men work along a wall from left to right.) A quick tap of the dry end of the brick against the top of the wall seats the mortar. The brick is then placed exactly where it is to rest (pushing it or picking it up and relaying it is an invitation to leaks in a pool). Trim away excess mortar and use that to butter the next brick.

It is best to build up corners first and then to work at the center section of a wall. Use a plumb level to keep in vertical alignment. Stretch fish line at each course to keep horizontal level.

Aquatic mosaics from pebbles and shells

Pebbles and shells go naturally with water, so what more appropriate use for them than in a garden pool? A decorative pattern not only brightens a pool, but shows the stones and shells at their best, for the water intensifies their colors while keeping surfaces clean.

Some craftsmen prefer to work out their designs first, as professionals do. But if children are involved in the project, or if the craftsman is attempting to achieve complete spontaneity, the pebbles can fall where they will, often with delightful results.

In either case, work goes quickest and smoothest if pieces are first separated by size and color (and by type if several materials are used).

Making small mosaics

The simplest way to embed the pebbles, glass, ceramic bits, or shells is to push them into the wet concrete soon after it is poured but before it sets. This works well if there are only a few pieces to place. (If the entire bottom and the walls of the pool are to be covered, the concrete will set before the work can be completed.)

After the shells, rocks, or mosaic tiles are in place, let the concrete harden for three or four hours. Then carefully wash excess concrete off the faces of the decorative pieces, using a gentle stream of water from the garden hose and a soft wire brush, or a broom.

For larger projects

When a large number of pieces is to be used in a pool mosaic, the best method is to set them in a layer of mortar spread over the cured concrete surface. Although the process keeps the project unfinished for a longer time and means more work, it at least has the advantage of waterproofing the pool thoroughly.

The concrete should be rough so there will be a good bond with the mortar. Work can be done, though, on a now-and-then basis. Each patch of mortar can be left to dry without your worrying about a firm bond developing between it and the next section.

First, wet down the concrete so it will not draw water from the mortar and cause it to dry too quickly. Then spread an inch-thick layer of mortar in a patch about a foot square.

Dip the decorative pieces in water (both to clean them and to wet them so they will not draw water from the mortar); then set them in place. As each foot-square patch is completed, spread another patch of mortar and continue. If the project is not finished in one day, mortar left over at the end of the day should be discarded before it sets. Start each new morning with a spanking fresh batch.

Experimentation is the only way to get the right mortar consistency. Consistency is of special importance if the wall of the pool is being decorated. If the mortar is too wet, it will slide to the bottom. If it is too dry, it will fail to hold the decorative pieces.

The usual recommendation is this: 1 part Portland cement, ½ part hydrated lime or lime putty, 4½ parts graded sand.

When the mortar has set, use a brush to clean off the faces of the pebbles, shells, glass bits, or whatever is used.

Mosaic *in grout can be done in small sections if size of pool makes sectioning necessary.*

Finished work *should look much like this. Individual pieces should make level floor; crevices should be minimal.*

Fountain head designs

Builders achieve strikingly different fountain effects with different heads as well as by lowering a head slightly below the water surface. It is a good idea, therefore, not to attach a fountain head so permanently that it cannot be changed.

Many fountain heads produce numerous fine sprays of water. These can be very attractive; they usually make little sound. Others, like the rotating head, throw droplets instead of spray.

Some heads simulate tulips, water lilies, or other plants. Both the lily pad ring B and the fountain ring A shown in the accompanying drawing are of the type that can be placed atop a waterproof 110-volt light fixture. A light inside the ring of spray is very effective. The new low-voltage swimming pool lights work in a garden pool.

Several inexpensive fountain heads can be fashioned from the brass fittings made for the pipe conduits of table lamps. The brass ¼-inch pipe is threaded full length. Knurled brass lock nuts fit it, as do plain and decorative caps in which one can drill spray holes.

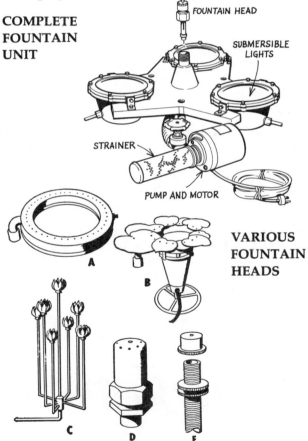

COMPLETE FOUNTAIN UNIT

FOUNTAIN HEAD

SUBMERSIBLE LIGHTS

STRAINER

PUMP AND MOTOR

VARIOUS FOUNTAIN HEADS

A

B

C

D

E

Top. *Commercially available fountain unit.* **A.** *Inverted spray head: 48 jets.* **B.** *Bronze lily pad ring over pool light.* **C.** *Bronze lilies, each with spray.* **D.** *Small fountain head: 10 jets.* **E.** *Brass lamp cap for vertical spray.*

Ways to light pools

Lighting gardens for night use is increasingly a part of outdoor living. And garden pools offer homeowners a ready focal point for garden lighting designs. In cases where the pool is to have a pump, lights can be added at the time the pump is installed at little cost.

For parties, a number of open-flame lights serve well. Luau torches cast dancing reflections across the surface of a pool, as do stubbier kerosene-fueled auto flares. Something as simple as candles floating on pieces of wood on the pool may create the mood a party hostess seeks.

Three basic approaches

When it is a matter of a permanent system, there are three basic approaches: submarine fixtures, ground-level highlighting, or overall illumination of the pool and its surroundings. The first two choices can be arranged for with either standard 115-volt circuitry or a low-voltage system. Low-voltage systems are often less expensive than standard ones. A general illumination scheme is most satisfactory if it uses 115-volt circuitry.

Circuit capacities. The average household circuit is a 15-ampere, 115-volt circuit. To the user, this means that its capacity is about 1,500 watts.

A man who is curious to know if an existing circuit will handle a larger load can quickly add up the present load; all light bulbs and electrical appliances have printed somewhere on them the watt power they require.

If the added power requirements of the pump and new lights still do not total 1,500 watts, no new circuit will be needed. Or if the total amount of watts likely to be in use at one time is less than 1,500, the present circuit will do.

Most garden pool pumps use between 50 and 100 watts of power; most outdoor lamps are 150 watts. A six-lamp system of low-voltage lights uses only 150 watts when operating at capacity.

Choosing a system. Versatility in a lighting system is sometimes an outright necessity, sometimes a handy convenience and sometimes no worry at all.

A main consideration is that the recirculating pump—where there is one—will require a grounded 115-volt outlet near the pool. Pumps come with a short length of approved waterproof cord and a grounded outdoor plug. Beyond that point, it is up to the pool's builder to get power to the pump.

Regular outdoor lamps can be part of the same circuit used by a pump, requiring only a separate switch and the necessary additional feet of wiring. If you do your own wiring, you will need a building permit and an inspector will check your work before approving it. Extra outlets can be installed to operate any electric tool outdoors.

Low-voltage circuits can tap off a regular circuit at any point. The primary concern with one of these kits is providing a weatherproof housing for the transformer. The system cannot power any lamp or appliance except the lamps which come as part of the kit.

Adding a low-voltage system to some existing circuit is less costly than augmenting an existing circuit and considerably less costly than wiring a new circuit into the service entry. If there is no need to add to the existing standard system, low voltage is the best bet. If it is necessary to add to the standard system, you can stay with 115 volts all the way at about the same initial cost but with higher operating costs.

Installing a circuit. All elements of an outdoor circuit should be purchased and installed with durability in mind. Municipal codes are unfailingly strict about the materials used. All outlets, switches, splice boxes, lamp sockets, and wires must be of approved weatherproof types. (Rainy days and damp nights are likely to cause short circuiting in improperly sealed connections.)

Outdoor cable must be either the direct-burial lead or neoprene type or be sheathed in rigid conduit when it is run underground. No. 14 cable is required on 15-ampere circuits with runs of 100 feet or less. No. 12 wire is used for longer runs or for circuits of higher amperage.

Either type of cable should be buried in a trench one shovel blade wide and 18 to 24 inches deep as a protection against accidental severing by some ground-breaking garden tool. If the trench must be shallower, the cable or conduit can be fastened with cable staples to the underside of 1 by 3-inch or 1 by 4-inch strips of redwood as a substitute protective device.

At any point where the cable leaves the ground, it must be protected either by rigid conduit or by flexible conduit secured to a wood post. In some instances the cable can be secured to a fence or screen post or to the pump housing for this purpose.

Sometimes it is desirable or necessary to run cable overhead. Most municipal codes require that overhead cable be sheathed in rigid conduit if it is 8 feet or less above the ground. Higher runs can be left exposed if they are passed through strain insulators (like those on utility pole cross-arms) at intervals of 15 feet. If the cable follows the trunk of a tree, it is advisable to save wear and tear on the insulation by encasing the cable in thin-wall tubing.

A weekend handyman himself may be able to do much of the groundwork for a system of this type, but all terminal connections should be made by a licensed electrician. Most municipalities require that the system be inspected before any of its cables are covered. Call for an inspection as soon as the electrician is finished to avoid any later difficulties with code requirements.

In purchasing light fixtures for above-water installation, be sure to get weather-resistant materials (aluminum, brass, copper, stainless steel, hard-finish plastics, ceramic clays). For underwater installation—whether fixtures cast into the pool shell, or "floating" fixtures—use only UL-approved types. Underwater is no place to have short circuits. For ease of installation, choose and buy underwater fixtures before beginning construction of the pool. Some types must be cast in the concrete.

Low-voltage systems. The standard low-voltage materials should include 100 feet of plastic-covered cable, 6 lamp units, and a transformer. The transformer is built to handle 6 additional lamps on a total of 200 feet of cable. Simple connectors permit the setting up of spur lines, but the total distance is still only 200 feet.

The transformer is wired directly into a standard circuit. On the other side of the transformer, above-grade lamps are attached to the cable sim-

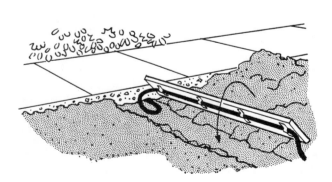

Underground cable *can be protected by attaching it to undersides of 1 by 3-inch scrap lumber.*

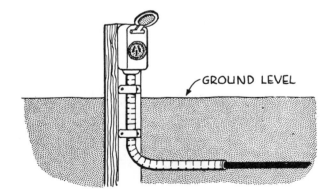

Outlets *at points where cable emerges from underground must be protected by rigid support.*

ply by slitting it and fitting the lamp housing onto the cable. Lamp housings that can be cast into pool shells or that float free in the water have short lead cables that attach to the main cable.

Main cables need be buried in as little as an inch or two of soil (nobody would be hurt by any short circuiting), but to protect the cables, attach them with brackets to 1 by 3-inch lumber in the same manner that standard circuits are attached. Use conduit where cable comes out of the ground.

Fire and water (*top left*) *make a dramatic combination. Here are kerosene-burning flare pots designed for use as safety flares for motorists. Lily pad reflectors* **(top right)** *softly illuminate pool; reflectors come equipped with waterproof cord and special socket. Plastic bowl* **(left)** *and commercial fountain were additions fitted into lighted walkway. Outdoor circuit suggested lighted fountain to owners.*

Index

Photographers

Ben J. Allen: 45 (bottom left). **Paul Aller:** 72, 73. **William Aplin:** 8 (bottom left), 10, 15 (bottom left, bottom right), 27 (top left), 29 (top left), 36, 46, 47 (bottom left), 55 (top left, top right, bottom left), 57 (top left), 59 (bottom left, bottom right). **Morley Baer:** 7 (bottom right), 45 (bottom right), 47 (bottom right), 50. **Baldinger Photo:** 16 (top). **Ernest Braun:** 7 (top left), 9 (top), 17 (top), 21 (top right), 29 (top right), 30, 31, 39 (bottom left), 40, 41 (bottom left), 45 (top), 76 (right). **Clyde Childress:** 14, 18 (left), 43 (bottom right), 62, 76 (left), 79 (top left). **Glenn M. Christiansen:** 8 (bottom right), 17 (bottom right), 61. **Robert Cox:** 13 (bottom right). **V. Davidson:** 12, 13 (all left and two top right). **Dearborn/Massar:** 38. **Max Eckert:** 48. **Richard Fish:** 4, 11 (bottom), 18 (top right, bottom right), 25 (bottom left), 35, 45 (center left), 51 (bottom). **Frank L. Gaynor:** 16 (bottom), 28. **Jeanette Grossman:** 25 (top left, top right). **Art Hupy:** 20, 24 (top left), 27 (bottom right). **Tats Ishimoto:** 15 (top right), 33 (top). **Elsa Knoll:** 55 (bottom right). **Samson B. Knoll:** 6, 41 (bottom right). **Roy Krell:** 64, 65 (top left). **Ells Marugg:** 22, 24 (top right), 42, 57 (bottom). **Jack McDowell:** 26, 41 (top left), 47 (top left), 51 (top right). **Ken Molino:** 27 (top right), 59 (top). **Don Normark:** 21 (top left, bottom), 51 (top left). **Theodore Osmundson:** 43 (bottom left), 54. **Rondal Partridge:** 47 (top right). **Chas. R. Pearson:** 8 (top left). **Norman A. Plate:** 52, 65 (bottom right). **Rain Jet:** 9 (bottom), 11 (top left, top right). **Tom Riley:** 7 (bottom left), 8 (top right), 29 (bottom). **John Robinson:** 41 (top right), 43 (top right), 60. **Julius Shulman:** 17 (bottom left). **William S. Stark:** 39 (top left). **William Steward:** 49. **George Taloumis:** 43 (top left). **Walter Tatsumi:** 65 (bottom left). **Darrow M. Watt:** 7 (top right), 15 (top left), 19, 27 (bottom left), 32, 33 (bottom), 34, 39 (top right, bottom right), 57 (top right), 65 (top right), 74. **R. Wenkam:** 79 (top right).